PLAGUE OF FROGS

Created by MIKE MIGNOLA

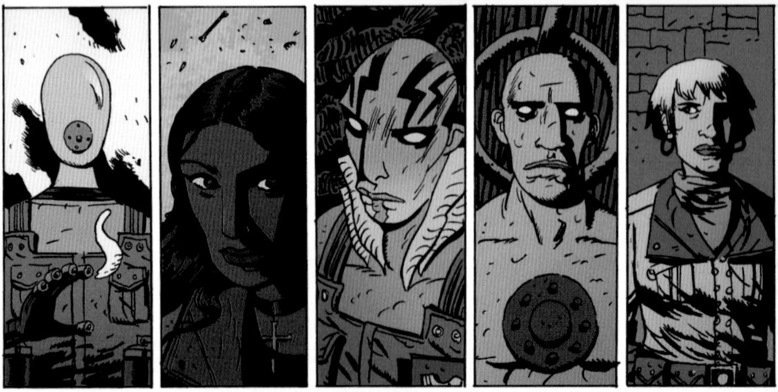

Johann Kraus

A medium whose physical form was destroyed while his ectoplasmic projection was out-of-body. That essence now resides in a containment suit. A psychic empath, Johann can create temporary forms for the dead to speak to the living.

Liz Sherman

A fire-starter since the age of 11, when she accidentally burned her entire family to death. She has been a ward of the B.P.R.D. since then, learning to control her pyrokinetic abilities and cope with the traumas those abilities have wrought.

Abe Sapien

An amphibious man discovered in a long-forgotten subbasement beneath a Washington, D.C. hospital sealed inside a primitive stasis chamber. All indications suggest a previous life, dating back to the Civil War—an unfolding mystery for Abe.

Roger

A homunculus made from human blood and herbs. Discovered in Romania, Roger was first brought to life by Liz's pyrokinetic touch. Whether or not he is actually alive may be up for debate, but his child-like love of that life is not.

Dr. Kate Corrigan

A former professor at New York University, an authority on folklore and occult history. Dr. Corrigan has been a B.P.R.D. consultant for over 10 years, now serving as special liaison to the enhanced-talents task force.

MIKE MIGNOLA'S

B.P.R.D.™

PLAGUE OF FROGS

TOM WEDDLE ♦ *vice president of finance*

RANDY STRADLEY ♦ *vice president of publishing*

CHRIS WARNER ♦ *senior books editor*

ANITA NELSON ♦ *vice president of sales & marketing*

MICHAEL MARTENS ♦ *vice president of business development*

DAVID SCROGGY ♦ *vice president of product development*

LIA RIBACCHI ♦ *art director*

DALE LaFOUNTAIN ♦ *vice president of information technology*

DARLENE VOGEL ♦ *director of purchasing*

KEN LIZZI ♦ *general counsel*

Published by Dark Horse Books
A division of Dark Horse Comics, Inc.
10956 SE Main Street
Milwaukie, OR 97222

First edition January 2005
ISBN: 1-59307-288-0

3 5 7 9 10 8 6 4 2

Printed in China

This book collects the *B.P.R.D. Plague of Frogs* issues 1-5, published by Dark Horse Comics.

Chapter One

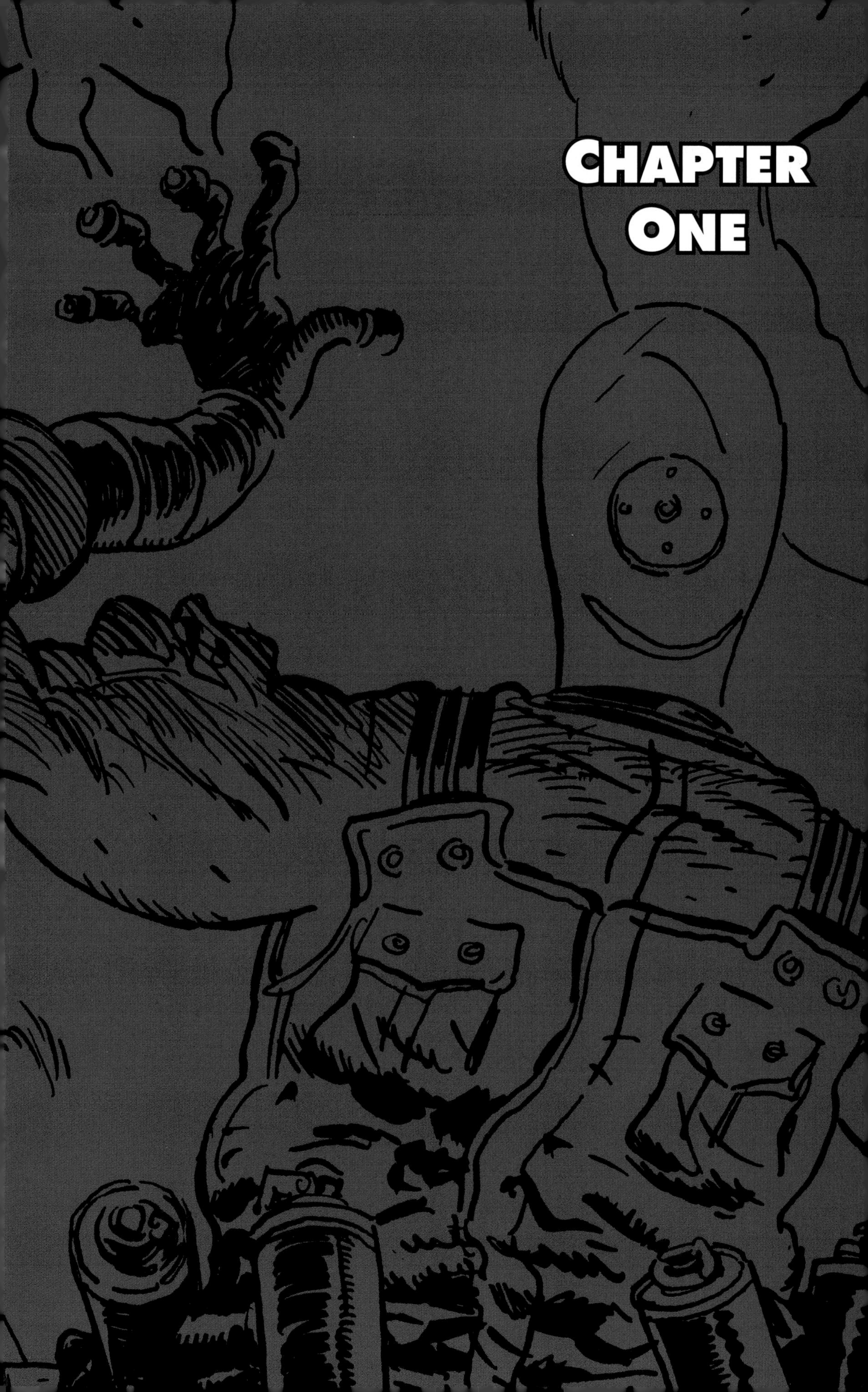

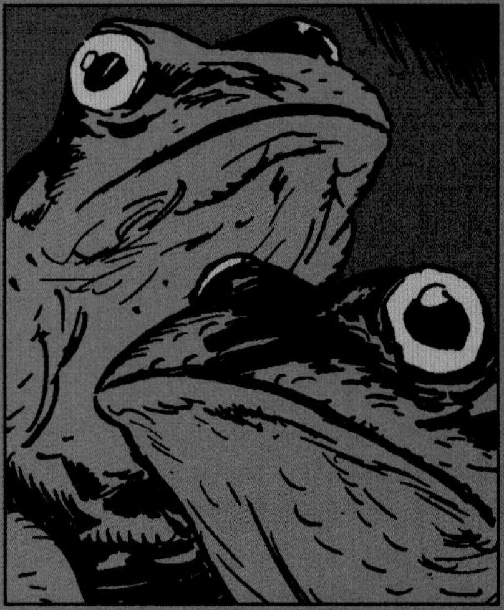

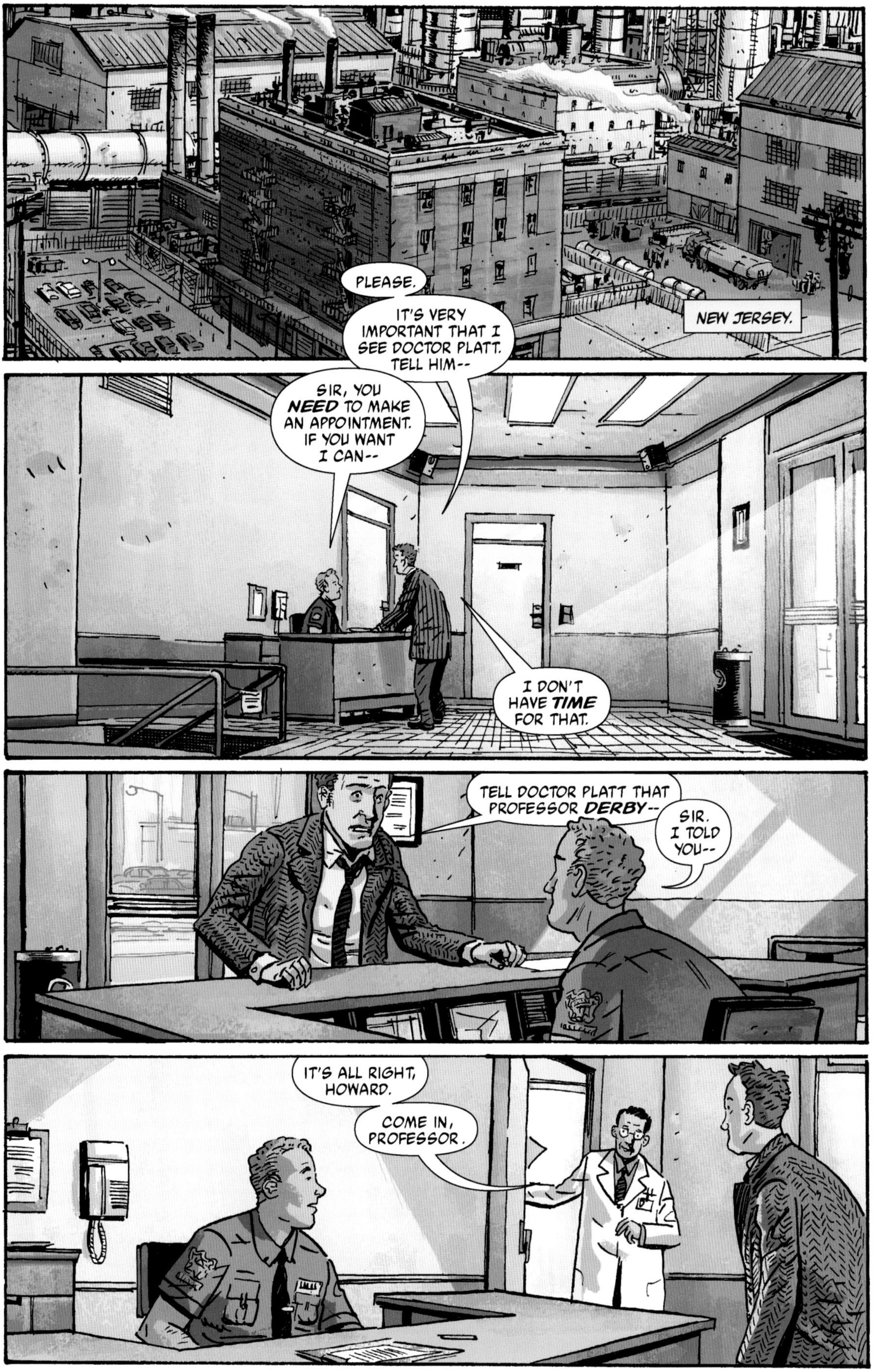
NEW JERSEY.
PLEASE.
IT'S VERY IMPORTANT THAT I SEE DOCTOR PLATT. TELL HIM--
SIR, YOU **NEED** TO MAKE AN APPOINTMENT. IF YOU WANT I CAN--
I DON'T HAVE ***TIME*** FOR THAT.
TELL DOCTOR PLATT THAT PROFESSOR ***DERBY***--
SIR. I TOLD YOU--
IT'S ALL RIGHT, HOWARD.
COME IN, PROFESSOR.

*BREAD MOLD

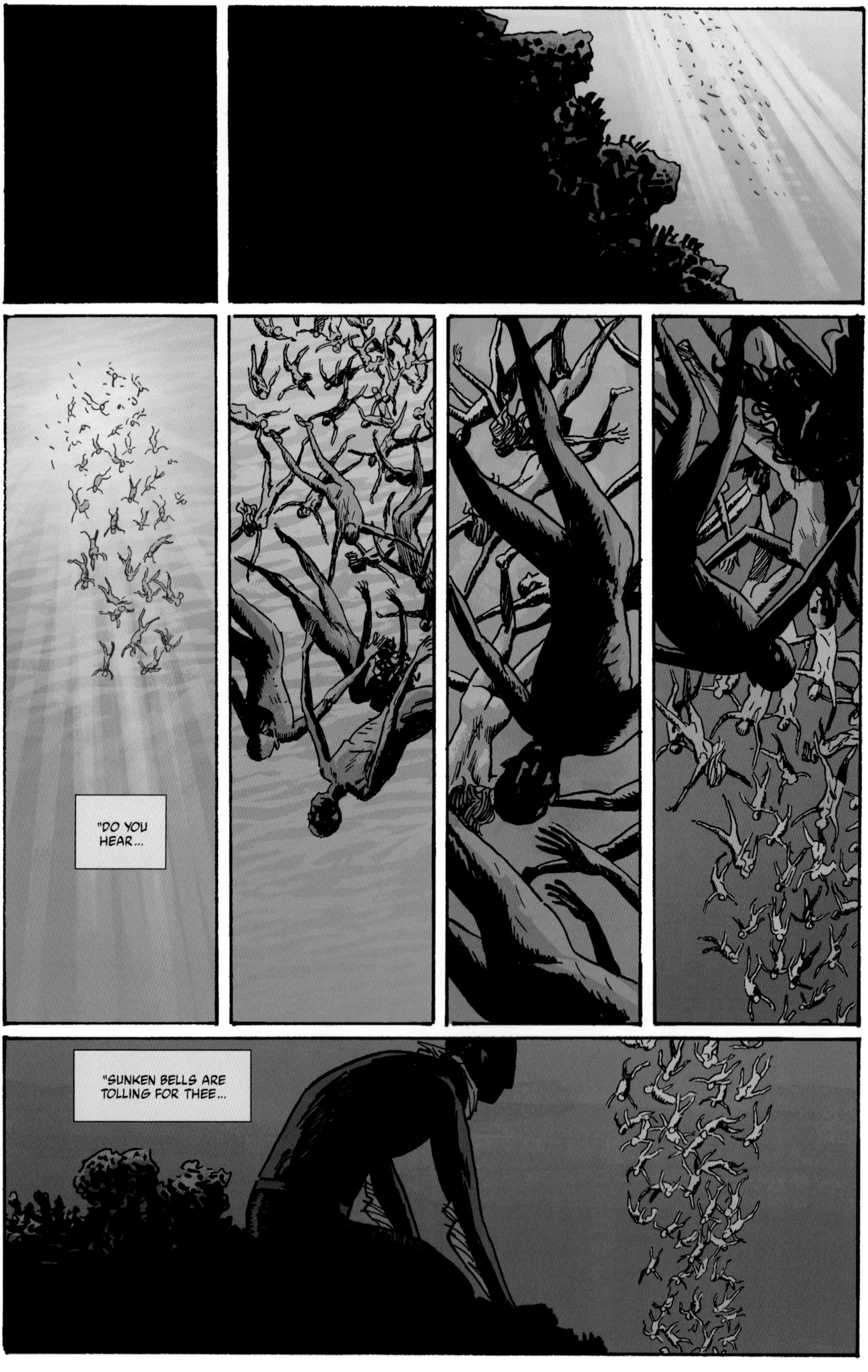
"DO YOU HEAR...
"SUNKEN BELLS ARE TOLLING FOR THEE...

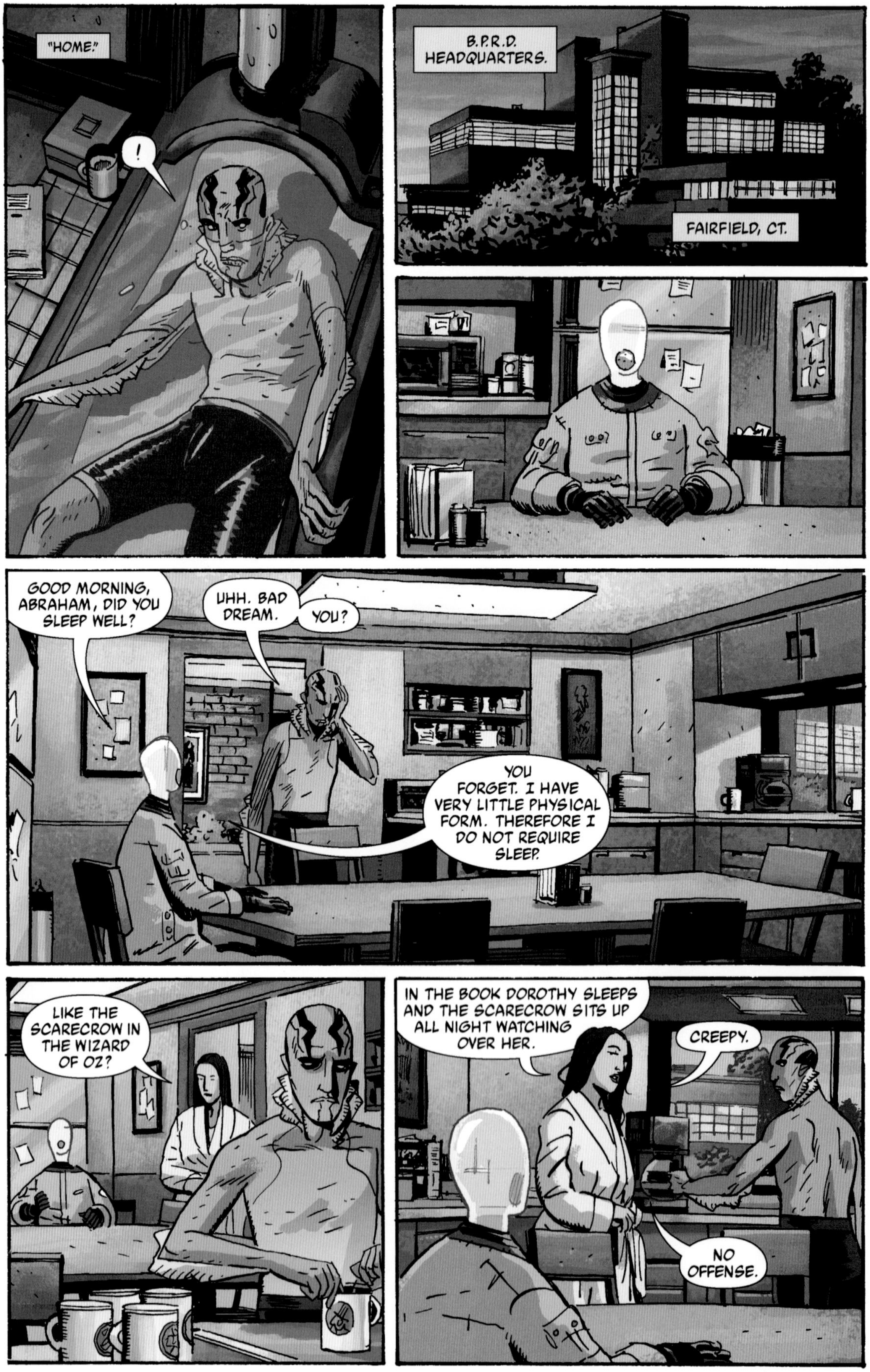
"HOME."
!
B.P.R.D. HEADQUARTERS.
FAIRFIELD, CT.
GOOD MORNING, ABRAHAM, DID YOU SLEEP WELL?
UHH. BAD DREAM.
YOU?
YOU FORGET. I HAVE VERY LITTLE PHYSICAL FORM. THEREFORE I DO NOT REQUIRE SLEEP.
LIKE THE SCARECROW IN THE WIZARD OF OZ?
IN THE BOOK DOROTHY SLEEPS AND THE SCARECROW SITS UP ALL NIGHT WATCHING OVER HER.
CREEPY.
NO OFFENSE.

NONE TAKEN.

I AM AWARE THAT MY UNIQUE CONDITION CAN BE... DISTURBING.

IT'S JUST THAT IT'S EARLY, JOHANN.

EVERYTHING'S A LITTLE DISTURBING BEFORE THE FIRST CUP OF COFFEE.

YOU SLEEP ALL RIGHT?

SURE...

AFTER TWO YEARS IN THAT MONASTERY MY THOUGHTS ARE SO WELL ORDERED... I DON'T DREAM AT ALL.

YOU GUYS SEEN ROGER?

GOOD MORNING, KATE. I THINK HE'S IN THE LIBRARY.

CLOACINA...

GRAB HIM. WE'RE GOING TO NEW JERSEY.

GREAAAT.

THE BUREAU'S BEEEN USING THIS PLACE SINCE THE '50S, MOSTLY TO WAREHOUSE STUFF THAT ISN'T *TECHNICALLY* SUPERNATURAL.

BUT STUFF THEY DON'T WANT THE PUBLIC TO KNOW ABOUT.

THAT'S RIGHT.

BUT THIS MORNING SOMEBODY GOT IN AND THERE WAS A SHOOTING.

SOUNDS LIKE A JOB FOR THE POLICE.

WUP WUP WUP

YEAH, WELL THEY KEEP SOME PRETTY WEIRD STUFF IN THERE.

UH HUHH...

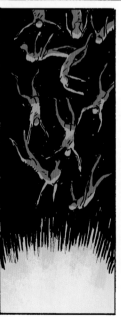

ABE. YOU OKAY?

SORRY...

ROUGH NIGHT?

BAD DREAM.

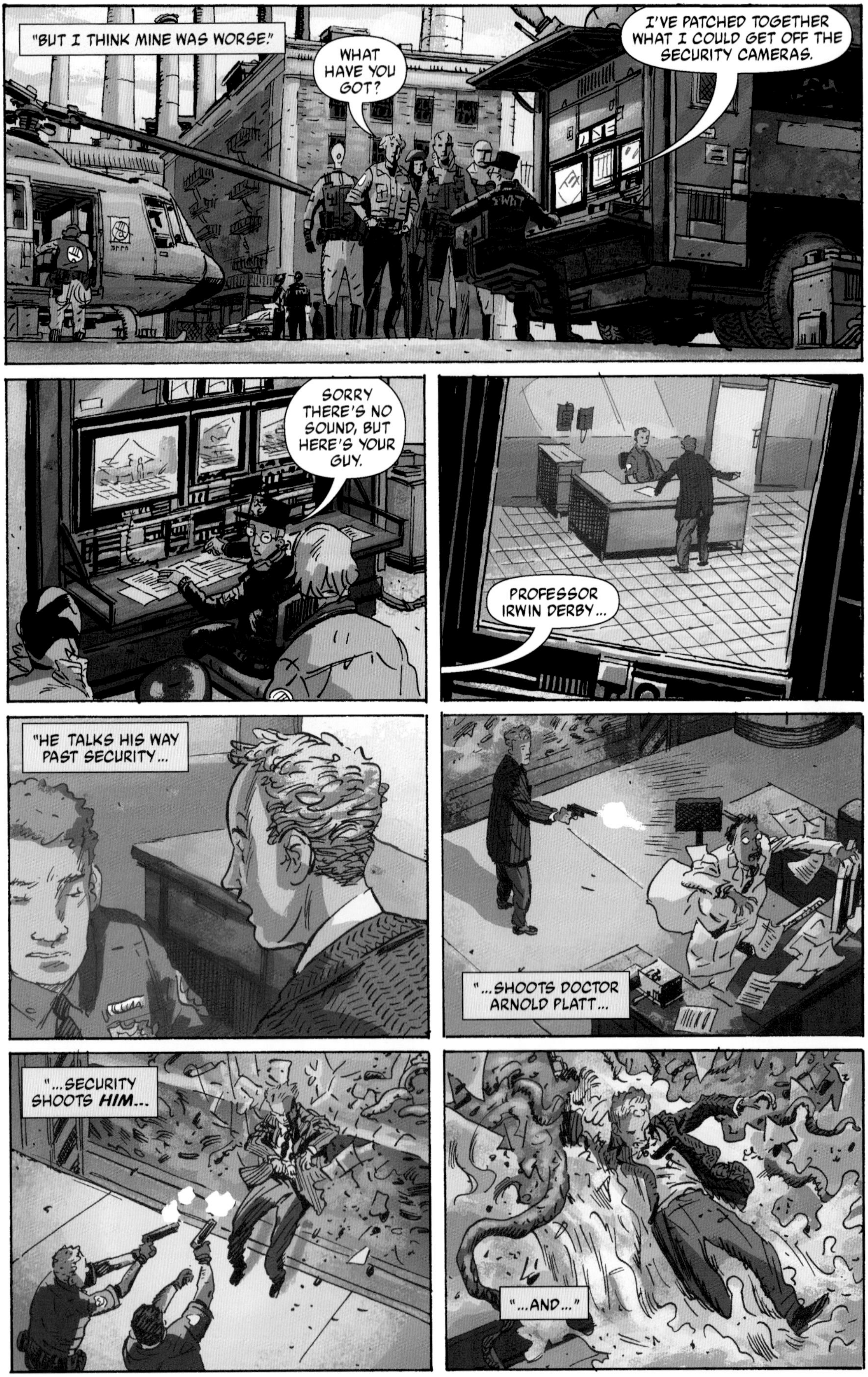
"BUT I THINK MINE WAS WORSE."
WHAT HAVE YOU GOT?
I'VE PATCHED TOGETHER WHAT I COULD GET OFF THE SECURITY CAMERAS.
SORRY THERE'S NO SOUND, BUT HERE'S YOUR GUY.
PROFESSOR IRWIN DERBY...
"HE TALKS HIS WAY PAST SECURITY...
"...SHOOTS DOCTOR ARNOLD PLATT...
"...SECURITY SHOOTS HIM...
"...AND..."

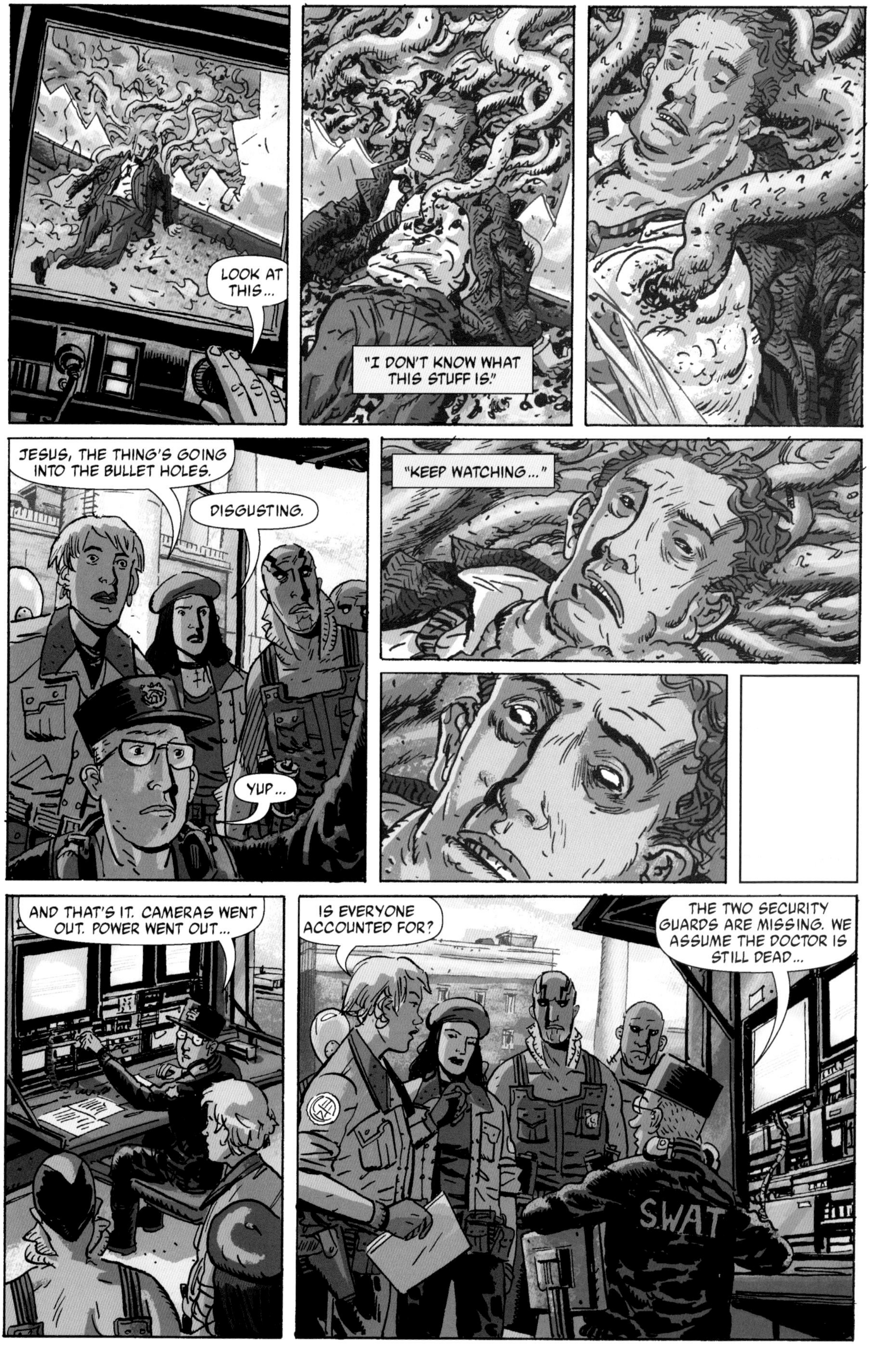
LOOK AT THIS...
"I DON'T KNOW WHAT THIS STUFF IS."
JESUS, THE THING'S GOING INTO THE BULLET HOLES.
DISGUSTING.
YUP...
"KEEP WATCHING..."
AND THAT'S IT. CAMERAS WENT OUT. POWER WENT OUT...
IS EVERYONE ACCOUNTED FOR?
THE TWO SECURITY GUARDS ARE MISSING. WE ASSUME THE DOCTOR IS STILL DEAD...
SWAT

"NO IDEA WHAT THE STORY IS WITH THE PROFESSOR."

BEEP

BEEP

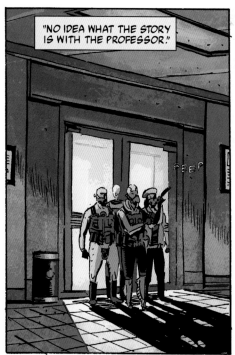

NOTHING IN THE AIR, JOHANN?

VIOLENCE... FEAR...

BUT NO TRACE OF HUMAN SPIRIT.

WHAT DOES THAT MEAN? NOBODY'S DEAD?

THAT'D BE SOMETHING...

"ROGER AND JOHANN--CHECK THE DOCTOR'S OFFICE."

WE'LL START DOWNSTAIRS.

YOU'RE THE BOSS.

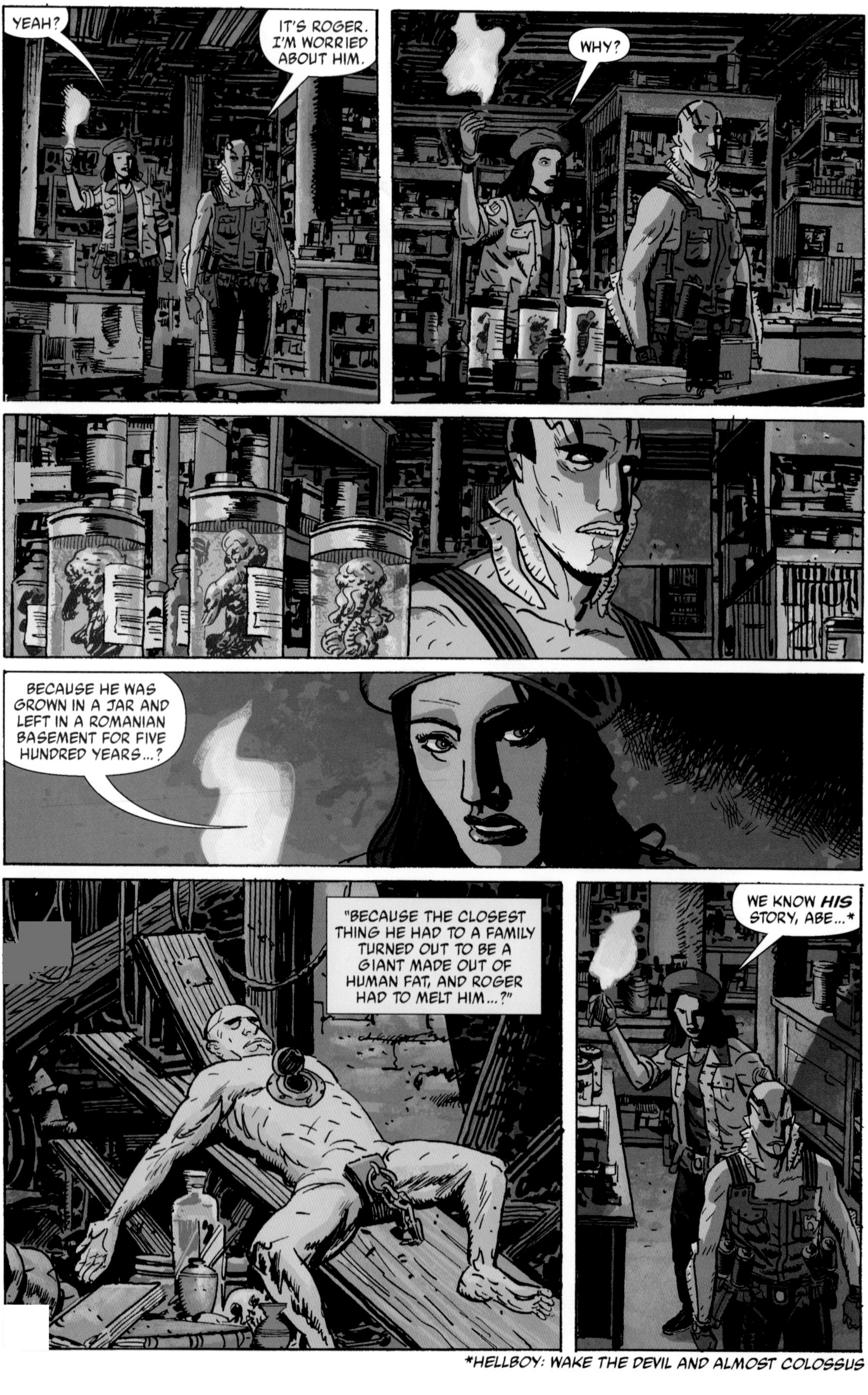
YEAH?
IT'S ROGER. I'M WORRIED ABOUT HIM.
WHY?
BECAUSE HE WAS GROWN IN A JAR AND LEFT IN A ROMANIAN BASEMENT FOR FIVE HUNDRED YEARS...?
"BECAUSE THE CLOSEST THING HE HAD TO A FAMILY TURNED OUT TO BE A GIANT MADE OUT OF HUMAN FAT, AND ROGER HAD TO MELT HIM...?"
WE KNOW **HIS** STORY, ABE...*

*HELLBOY: WAKE THE DEVIL AND ALMOST COLOSSUS

"WE KNOW *JOHANN'S* STORY*..."

"WE KNOW *MY* STORY**..."

I GUESS THE ONLY GUY WHOSE STORY WE *DON'T* KNOW IS YOU.

WHAT ARE YOU DREAMING ABOUT, ABE?

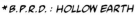

*B.P.R.D.: HOLLOW EARTH   **HELLBOY: SEED OF DESTRUCTION

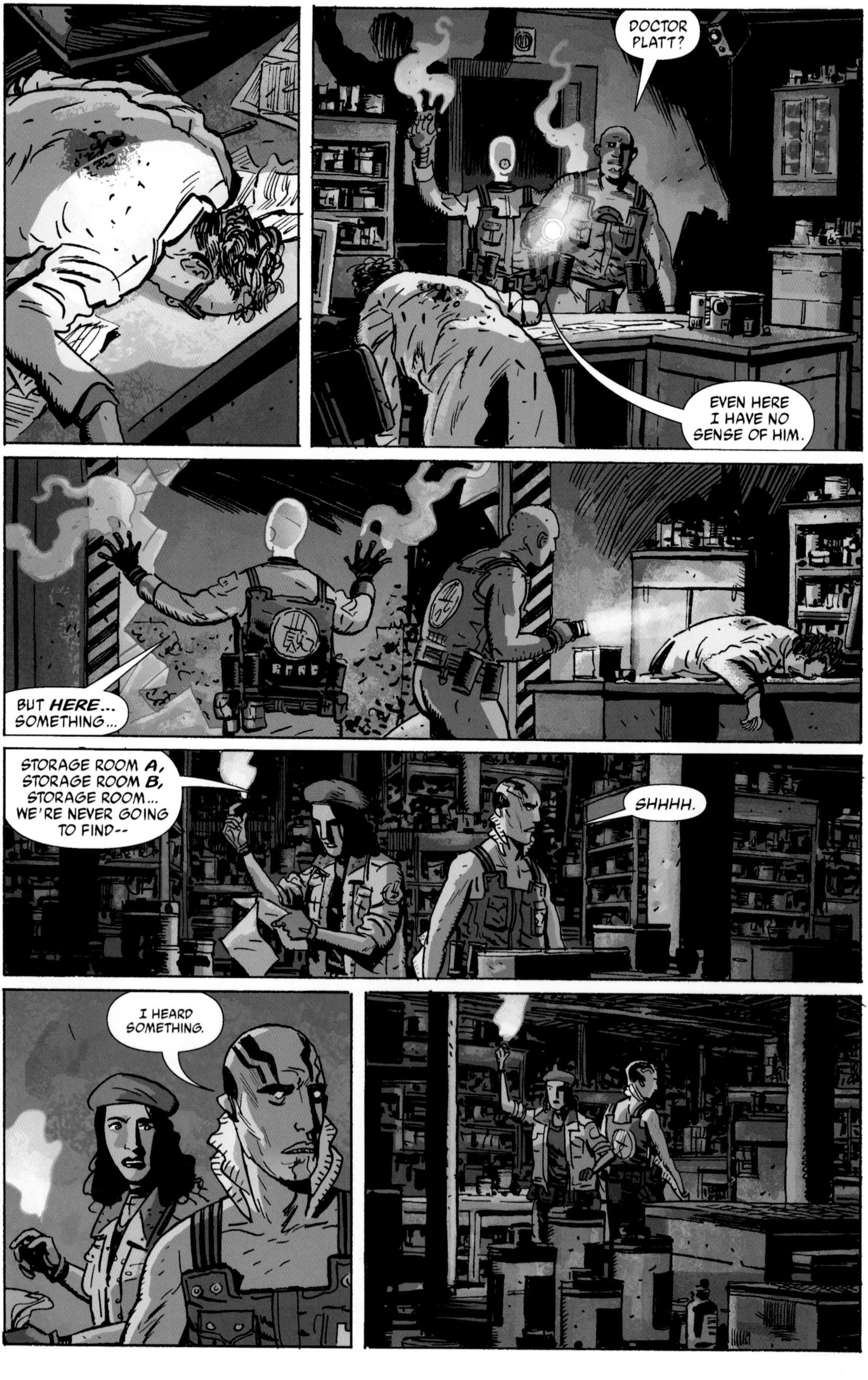

DOCTOR PLATT?
EVEN HERE I HAVE NO SENSE OF HIM.
BUT HERE... SOMETHING...
BPRD
STORAGE ROOM A, STORAGE ROOM B, STORAGE ROOM... WE'RE NEVER GOING TO FIND--
SHHHH.
I HEARD SOMETHING.

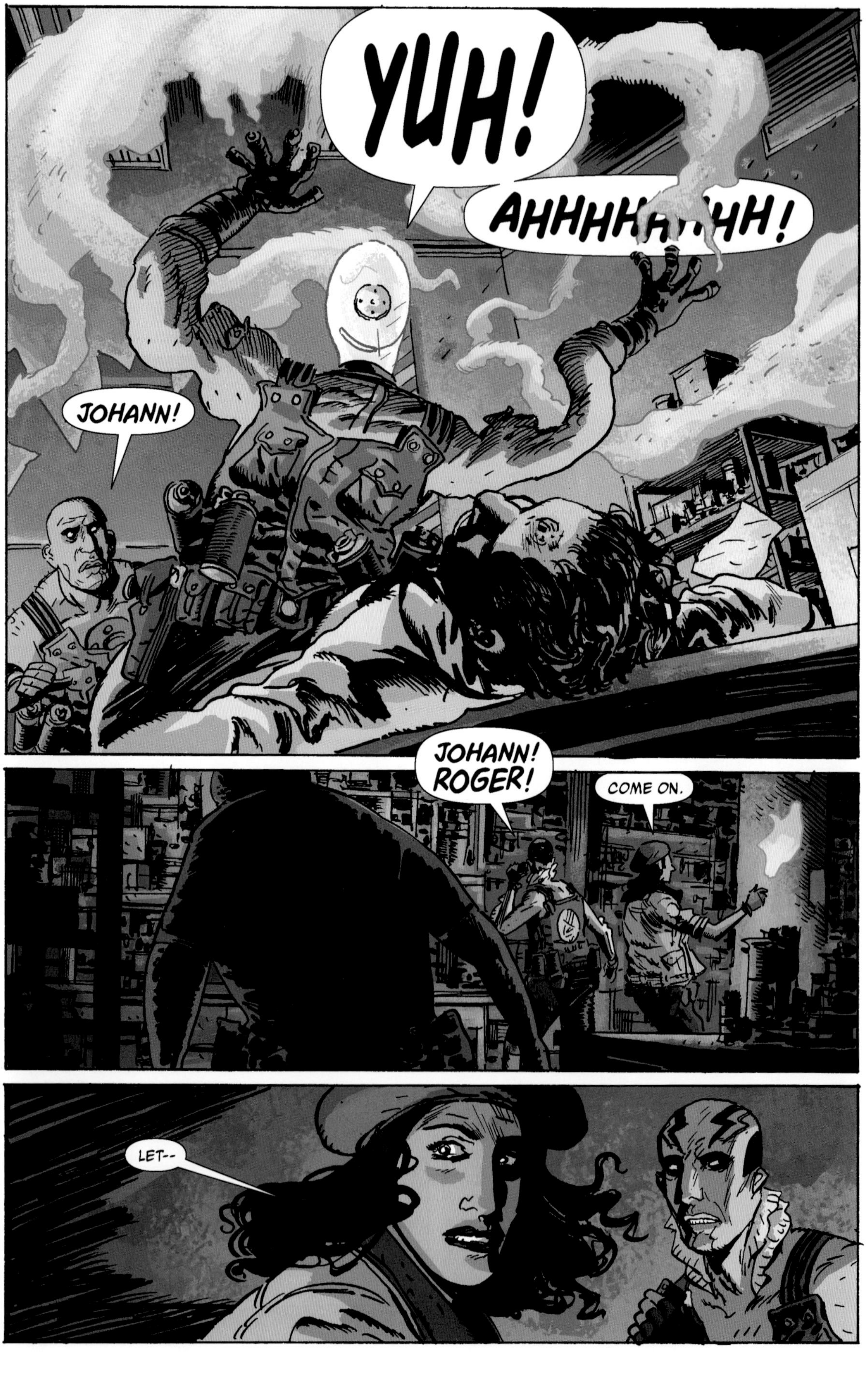
YUH!
AHHHHHHHH!
JOHANN!
JOHANN! ROGER!
COME ON.
LET--

AAAARP

AAAARRRP

LIZ!

UGH!

ABE, GET OUT OF THE WAY!

LIZ!

I'LL COOK HIM-- JUST GET OUT OF--

RAARP

AAH!

SON OF A...

...

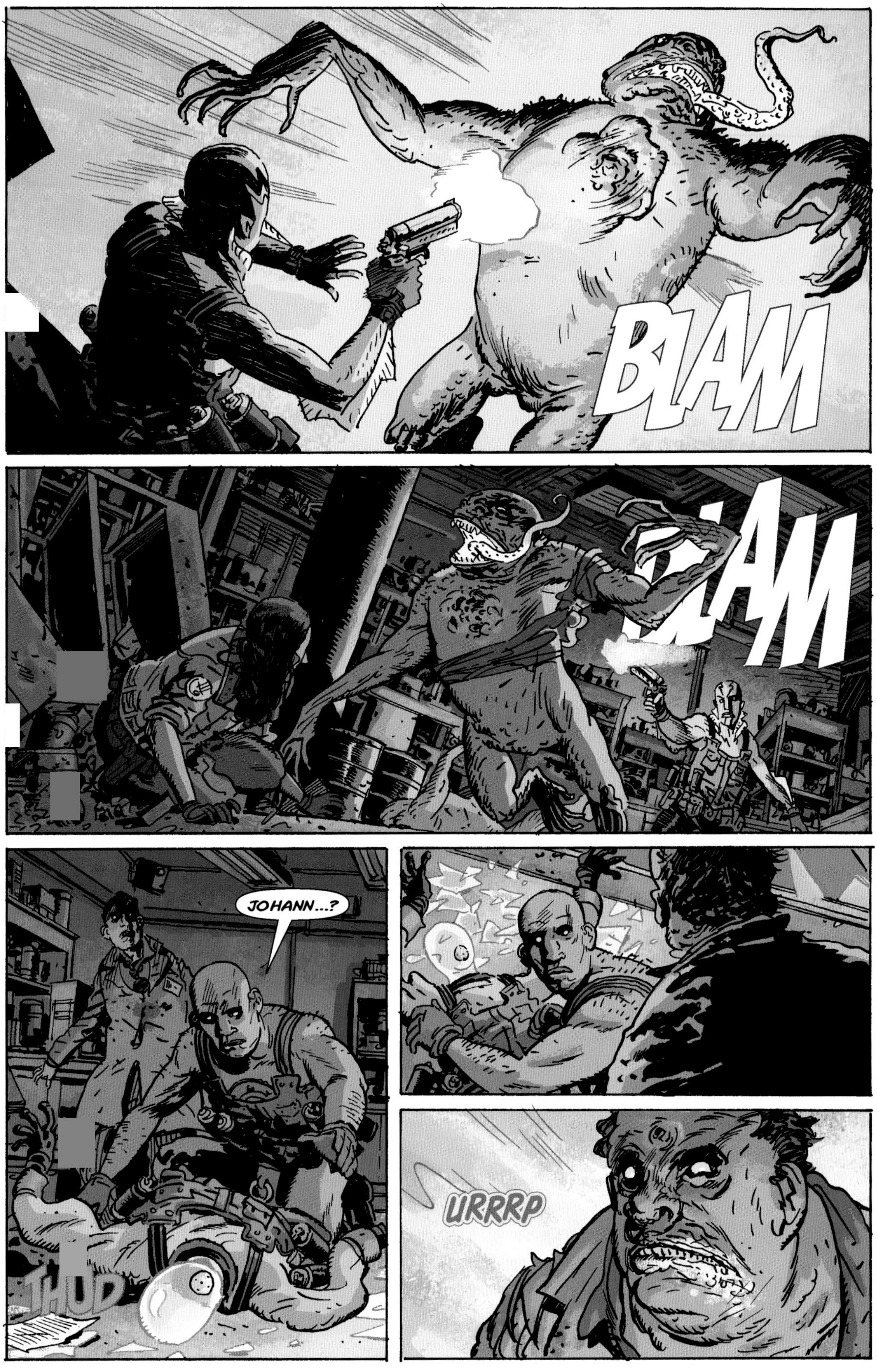
BLAM
BLAM
JOHANN...?
THUD
URRRP

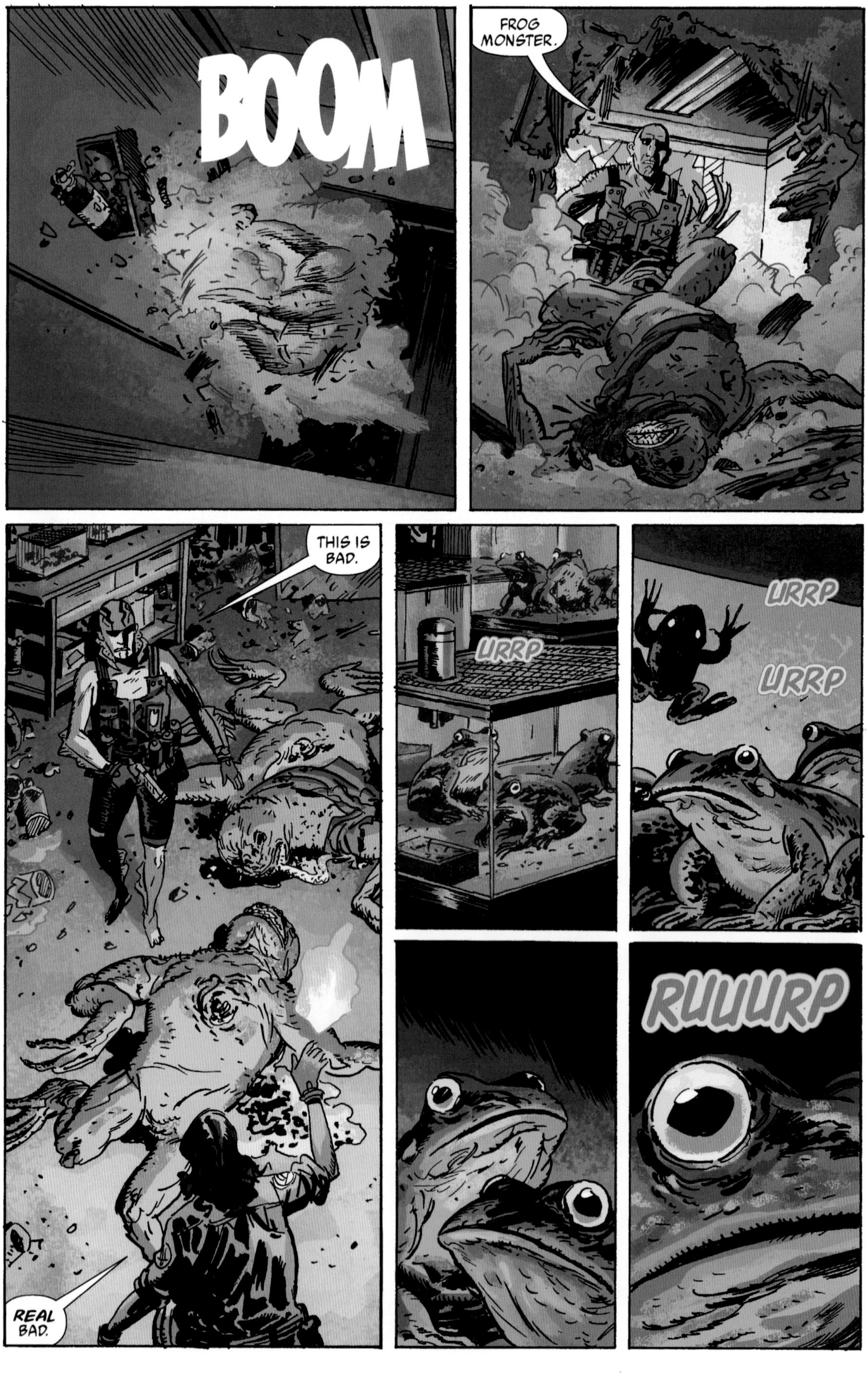
BOOM
FROG MONSTER.
THIS IS BAD.
REAL BAD.
URRP
URRP
URRP
RUUURP

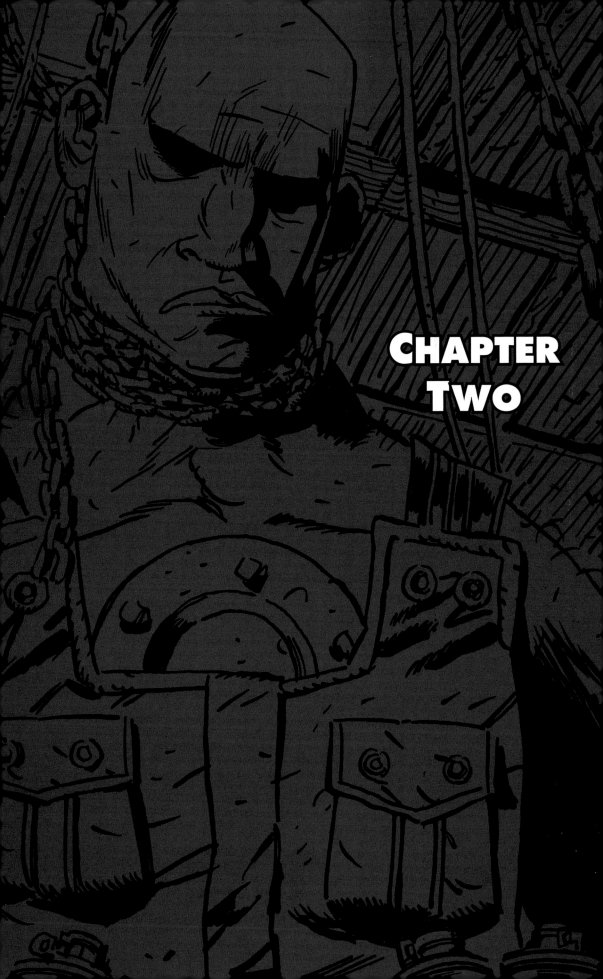

CHAPTER
TWO

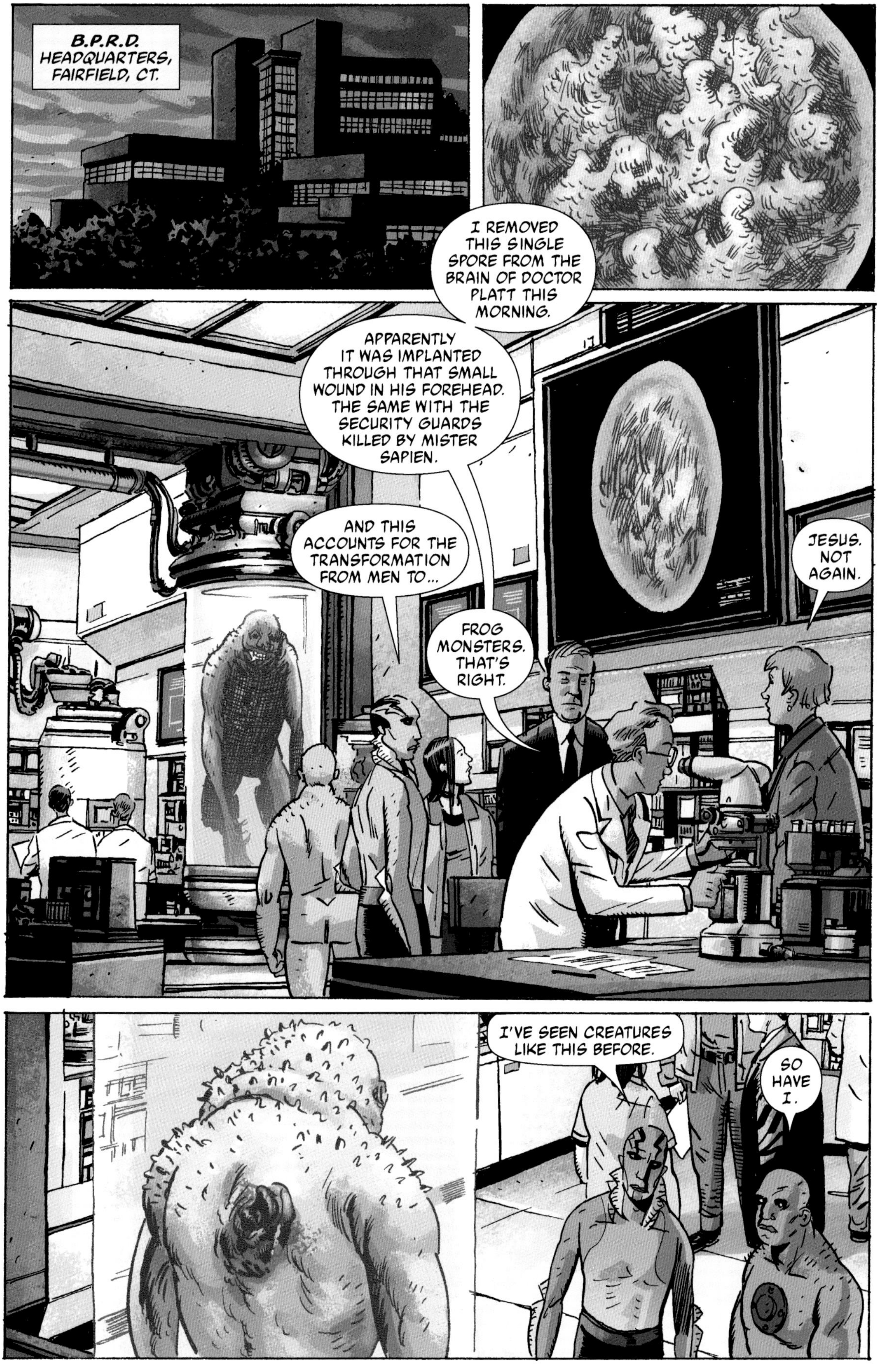
B.P.R.D. HEADQUARTERS, FAIRFIELD, CT.
I REMOVED THIS SINGLE SPORE FROM THE BRAIN OF DOCTOR PLATT THIS MORNING.
APPARENTLY IT WAS IMPLANTED THROUGH THAT SMALL WOUND IN HIS FOREHEAD. THE SAME WITH THE SECURITY GUARDS KILLED BY MISTER SAPIEN.
AND THIS ACCOUNTS FOR THE TRANSFORMATION FROM MEN TO...
FROG MONSTERS. THAT'S RIGHT.
JESUS. NOT AGAIN.
I'VE SEEN CREATURES LIKE THIS BEFORE.
SO HAVE I.

CAVENDISH HALL...

"THE THREE CAVENDISH BROTHERS. I SAW TWO OF THEM IN THE BASEMENT WITH THEIR DEAD MOTHER...

"WE ASSUME THEY WERE KILLED WHEN THE HOUSE WAS DESTROYED."

AND DON'T FORGET THE *THIRD* BROTHER.

HE KILLED PROFESSOR BRUTTENHOLM, AND HELLBOY SHOT HIM TRYING TO ESCAPE OUT A BATHROOM WINDOW.

HELLBOY...

I MISS HIM.

YEAH, WELL...

SADU-HEM!*

ACCORDING TO RASPUTIN, THE CAVENDISH BROTHERS AND THAT OTHER GUY, OLAFSON, GOT INFECTED BY THAT THING HE BROUGHT DOWN FROM THE ARCTIC--SADU-WHAT'S-HIS-NAME.

HELLBOY AND I FOUND SIMILAR CREATURES AT HUNTE CASTLE, CREATED BY GAS FROM A SPACE CAPSULE.**

SADU-HEM!

PROFESSOR O'DONNELL?

*HELLBOY: SEED OF DESTRUCTION
**HELLBOY: CONQUEROR WORM

PROFESSOR--

IT *IS* SADU-HEM! *IBISH ET EBB SADU-HEM!*

CALM DOWN, PROFESSOR.

I WARNED YOU, MANNING. I *WARNED* YOU. AND NOW IT'S FREE, AND IT'S INSIDE THIS MAN DERBY AND IT'S OUT THERE AND--

GET A HOLD OF YOURSELF, PROFESSOR.

I TOLD YOU TO DESTROY IT WHEN YOU HAD THE CHANCE!

TOM?

YOU KNOW BUREAU PROCEDURE, KATE.

EVERY SIX MONTHS WE DO A FOLLOW-UP INVESTIGATION IN THE CAVENDISH HALL RUINS...

"FOR TEN YEARS THERE'S NEVER BEEN ANY SIGN OF LIFE...

"THEN SIX WEEKS AGO..."

BEEEEP

WHAT IS THAT?

"A TINY BIT OF PLANT MATERIAL. A FUNGUS...

"WE SECURED IT...

"...MOVED IT TO THE NEW JERSEY LAB...

"...AND ALLOWED IT TO GROW."

FOOL.

HINDSIGHT IS, OF COURSE, 20/20. WE FELT THE OBJECT WAS PROPERLY CONTAINED, AND FROM A SCIENTIFIC STAND-POINT...THE WHOLE *GROWING THING* SEEMED LIKE A GOOD IDEA AT THE TIME.

YOU THOUGHT THAT HE WAS DESTROYED? NOOOOO. HE HAS RESURRECTED HIMSELF. OUT OF THE MUCK AND THE SLIME--AS HE WAS SPAWNED IN THE BEGINNING, AND ALL HIS BRETHREN AND ALL HIS MASTERS.

NOW HE HIDES HIMSELF INSIDE A HUMAN SKIN AND GOES FORTH IN THE WORLD... LIKE A MAN.

IT IS WRITTEN, "HE WHO WAS LAST TO SLEEP SHALL BE THE FIRST TO WAKE, AND LEAVE ALL FOUL THINGS TO THE EARTH. TROUBLE THEM NOT IN THEIR HOLES AND THEIR PRISONS.

"AND MOSTLY AND FIRSTLY, BEWARE OF *HIM*, FOR HIS BOWL IS FORGED OF COFFIN NAILS AND MADE IN THE SHAPE OF A SKULL...

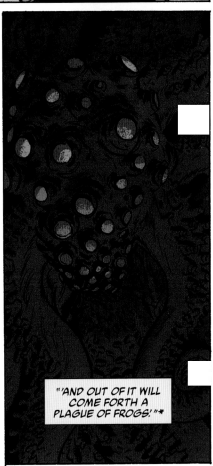

"'AND OUT OF IT WILL COME FORTH A PLAGUE OF FROGS!'"*

*HANS WERNER SCHLEGEL, NUREMBERG 1632

ALL RIGHT, PROFESSOR. ALL RIGHT...

LET'S SEE IF WE CAN FIND YOUR PILLS.

ANY WORD ON THIS GUY DERBY?

WELL, THEY DIDN'T FIND HIS BODY AT THE LAB, BUT THEY *DID* FIND A BIG HOLE IN THE FLOOR, AND A TUNNEL LEADING DOWN TO THE PATH TRAIN...

SO HE COULD BE ANY-WHERE.

WHAT DO WE KNOW ABOUT HIM?

NOT MUCH SO FAR. HE WAS A PROFESSOR AT CORNELL, BUT A COUPLE WEEKS AGO HE JUST UP AND QUIT.

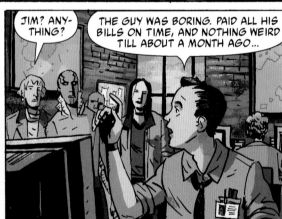

JIM? ANY-THING?

THE GUY WAS BORING. PAID ALL HIS BILLS ON TIME, AND NOTHING WEIRD TILL ABOUT A MONTH AGO...

THEN HE STARTED WRITING BIG CHECKS TO SOMETHING CALLED *"THE NEW TEMPLE OF MYSTERIES."*

THE WHAT?

WHERE'S THAT?

CRAB POINT, MICHIGAN.

WUP WUP WUP WUP WUP WUP WUP

DOESN'T LOOK LIKE ANYBODY'S HOME.

NOPE.

GARAGE

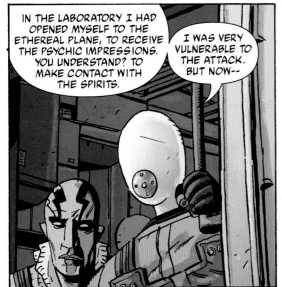

IN THE LABORATORY I HAD OPENED MYSELF TO THE ETHEREAL PLANE, TO RECEIVE THE PSYCHIC IMPRESSIONS. YOU UNDERSTAND? TO MAKE CONTACT WITH THE SPIRITS.

I WAS VERY VULNERABLE TO THE ATTACK. BUT NOW--

WAIT.

THERE.

WUP WUP WUP

YOU SEE, I SENSE THE ALIEN PRESENCE, BUT I AM PREPARED. I--

GAAAA!

I'VE GOT YOU.

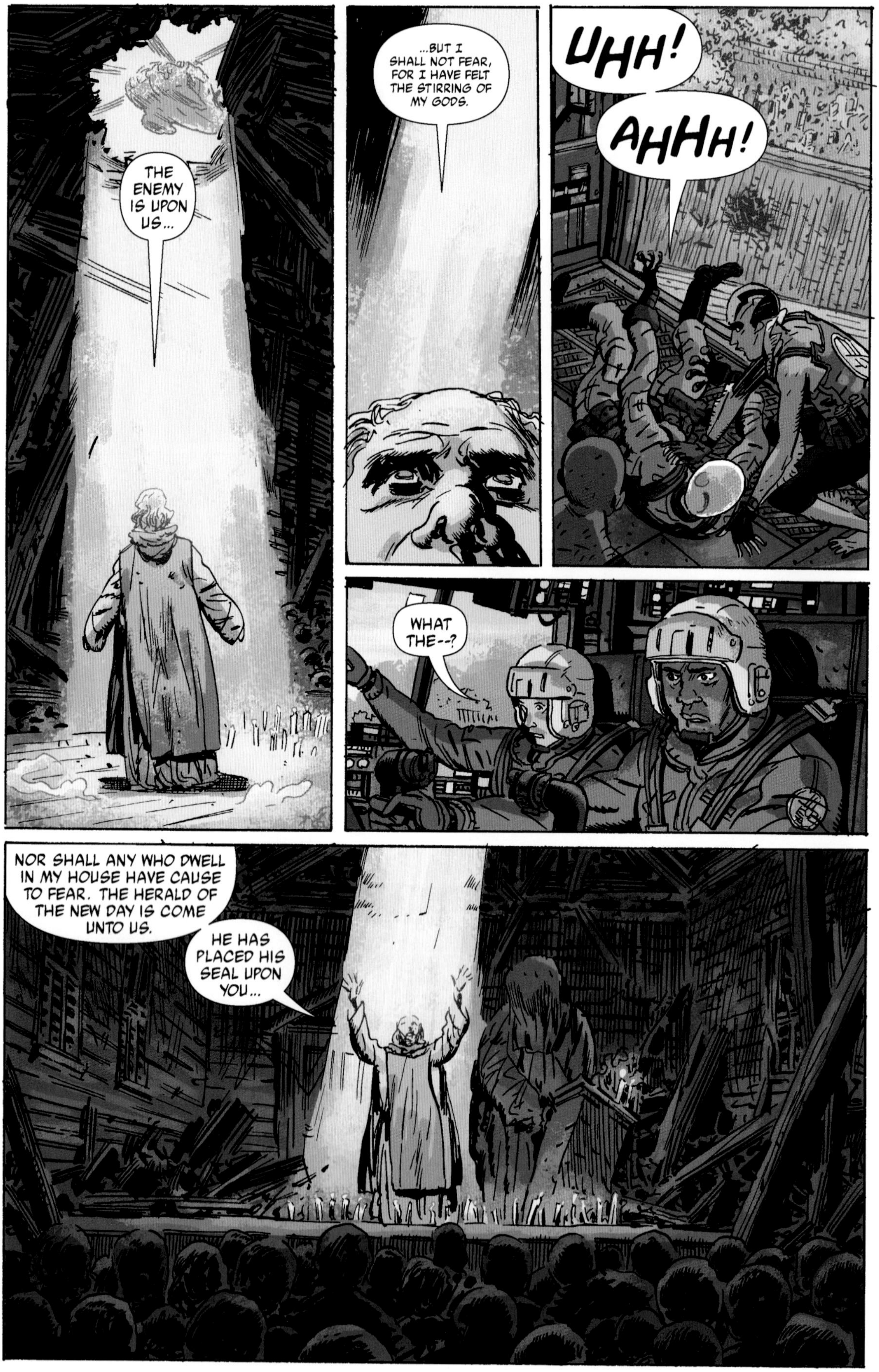
THE ENEMY IS UPON US...
...BUT I SHALL NOT FEAR, FOR I HAVE FELT THE STIRRING OF MY GODS.
UHH!
AHHH!
WHAT THE--?
NOR SHALL ANY WHO DWELL IN MY HOUSE HAVE CAUSE TO FEAR. THE HERALD OF THE NEW DAY IS COME UNTO US.
HE HAS PLACED HIS SEAL UPON YOU...

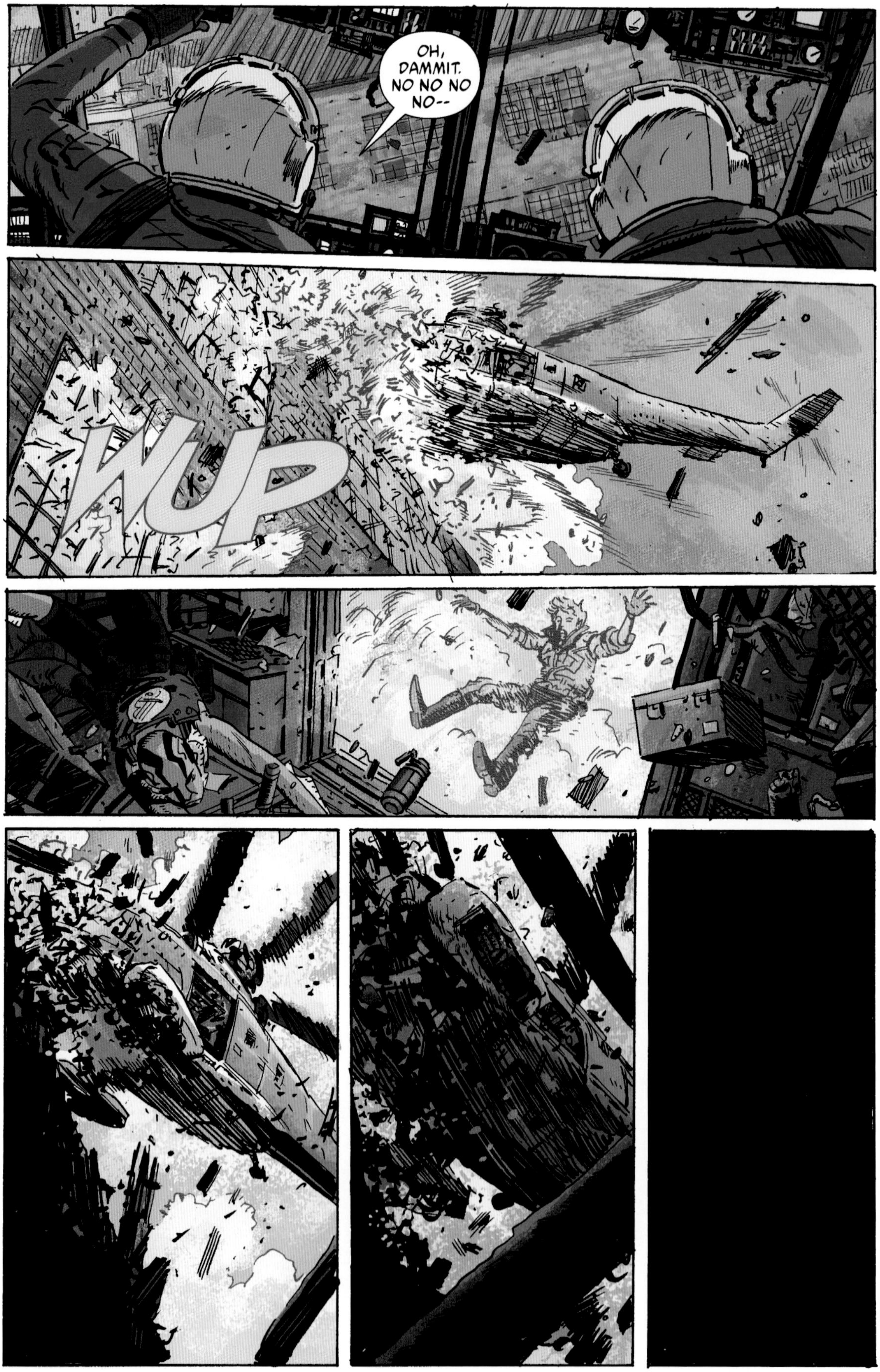
OH, DAMMIT. NO NO NO NO--
WUP

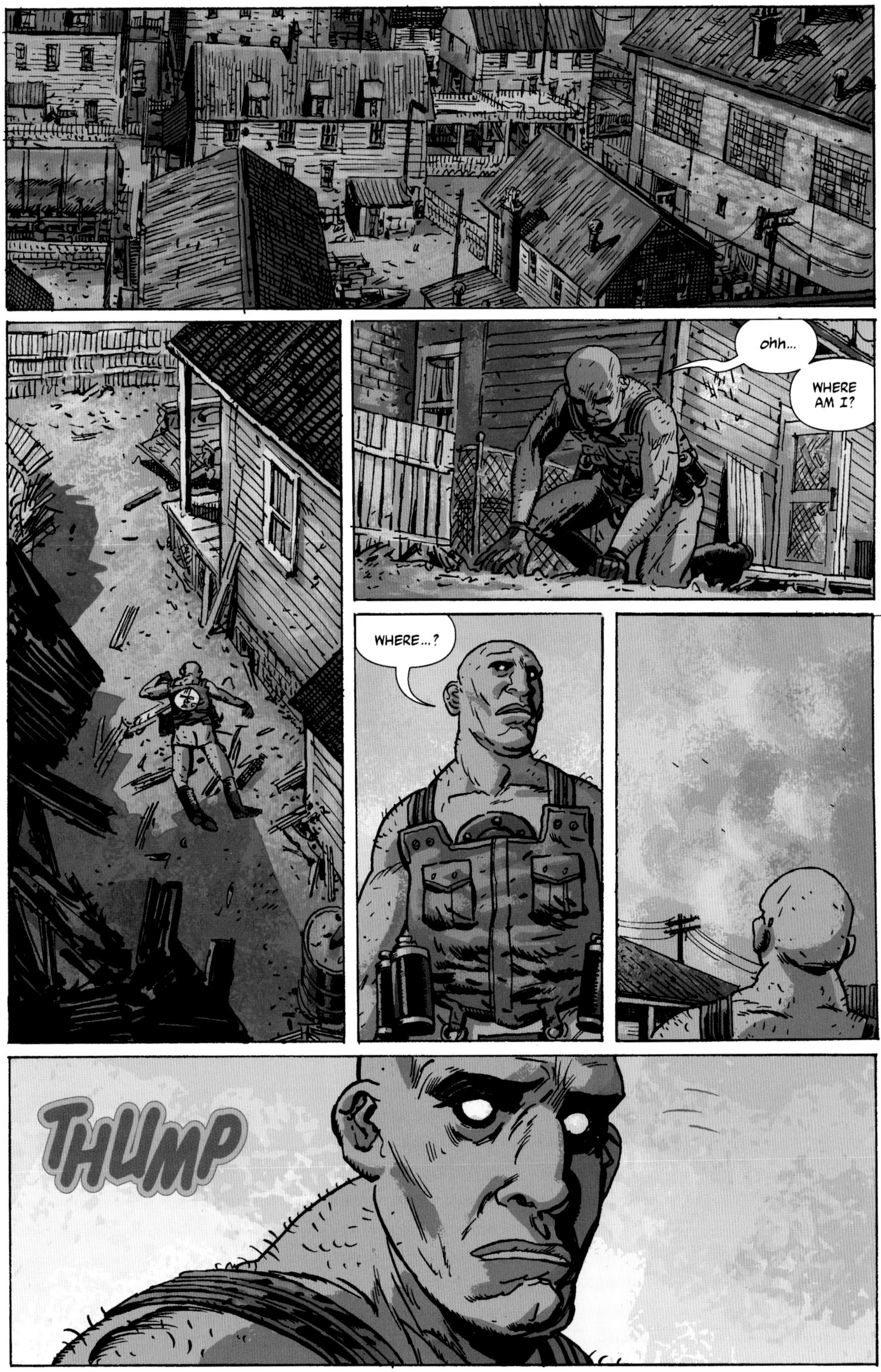
ohh...
WHERE AM I?
WHERE...?
THUMP

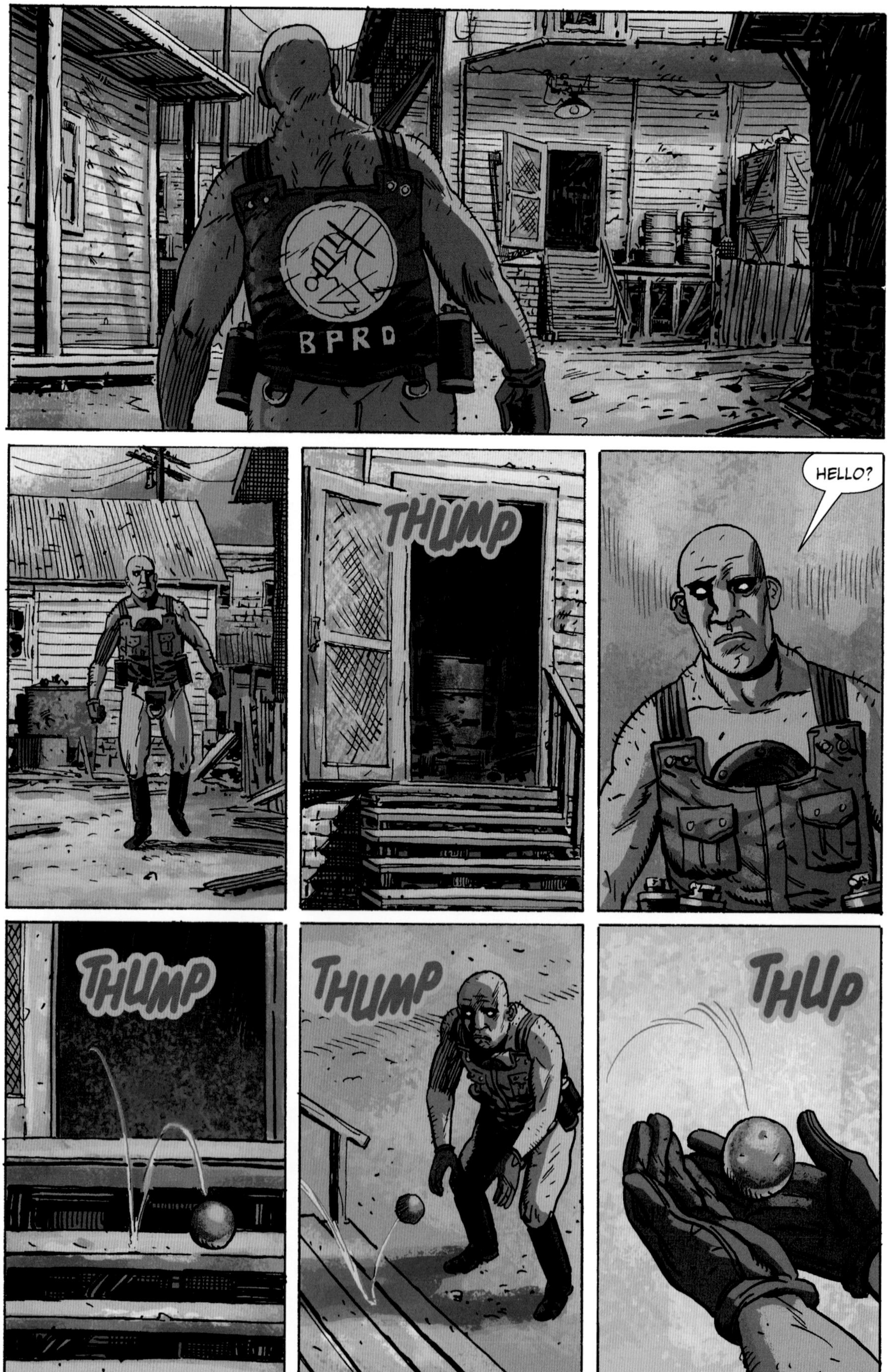
BPRD
THUMP
HELLO?
THUMP
THUMP
THUP

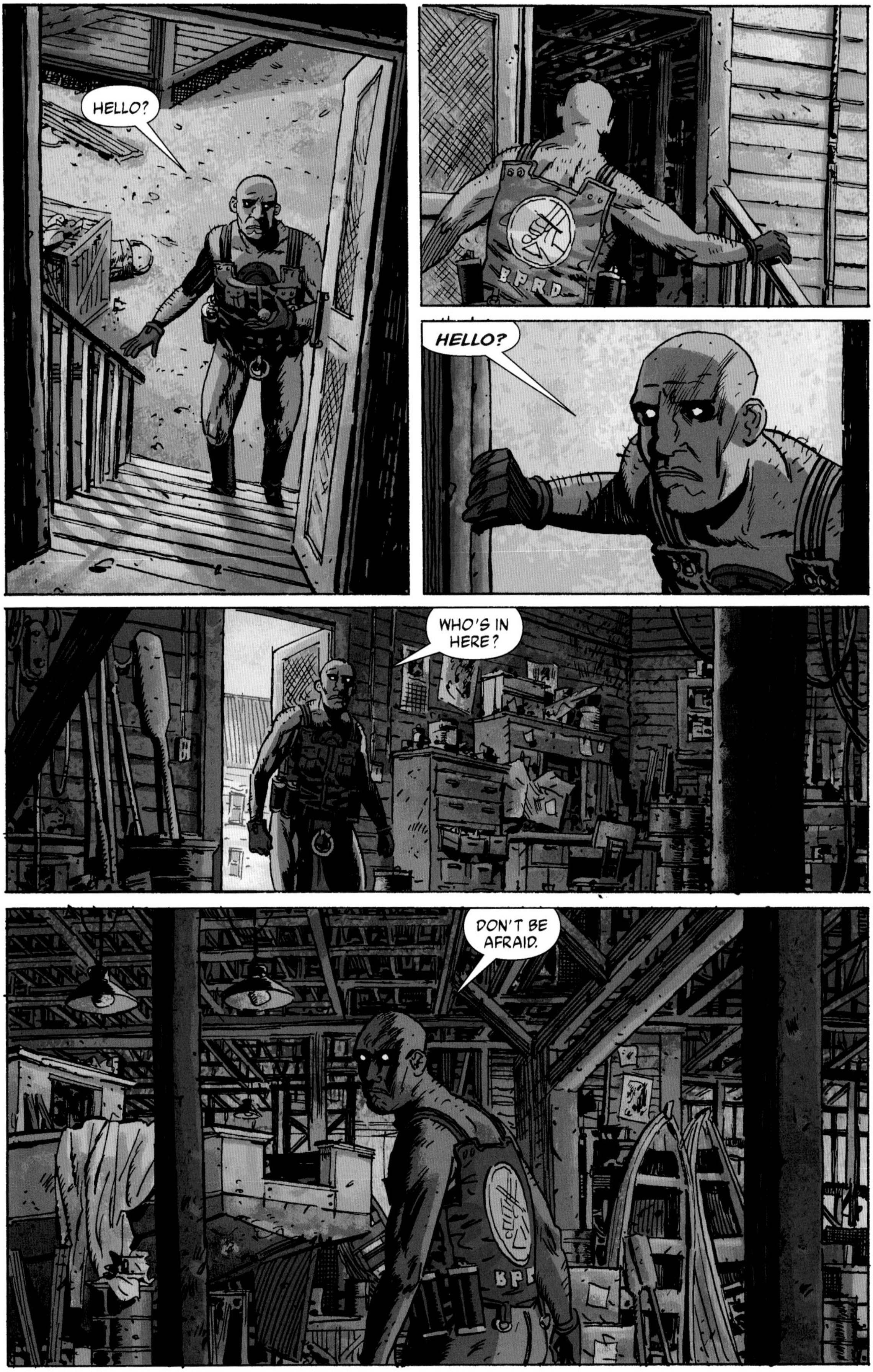
HELLO?
HELLO?
WHO'S IN HERE?
DON'T BE AFRAID.

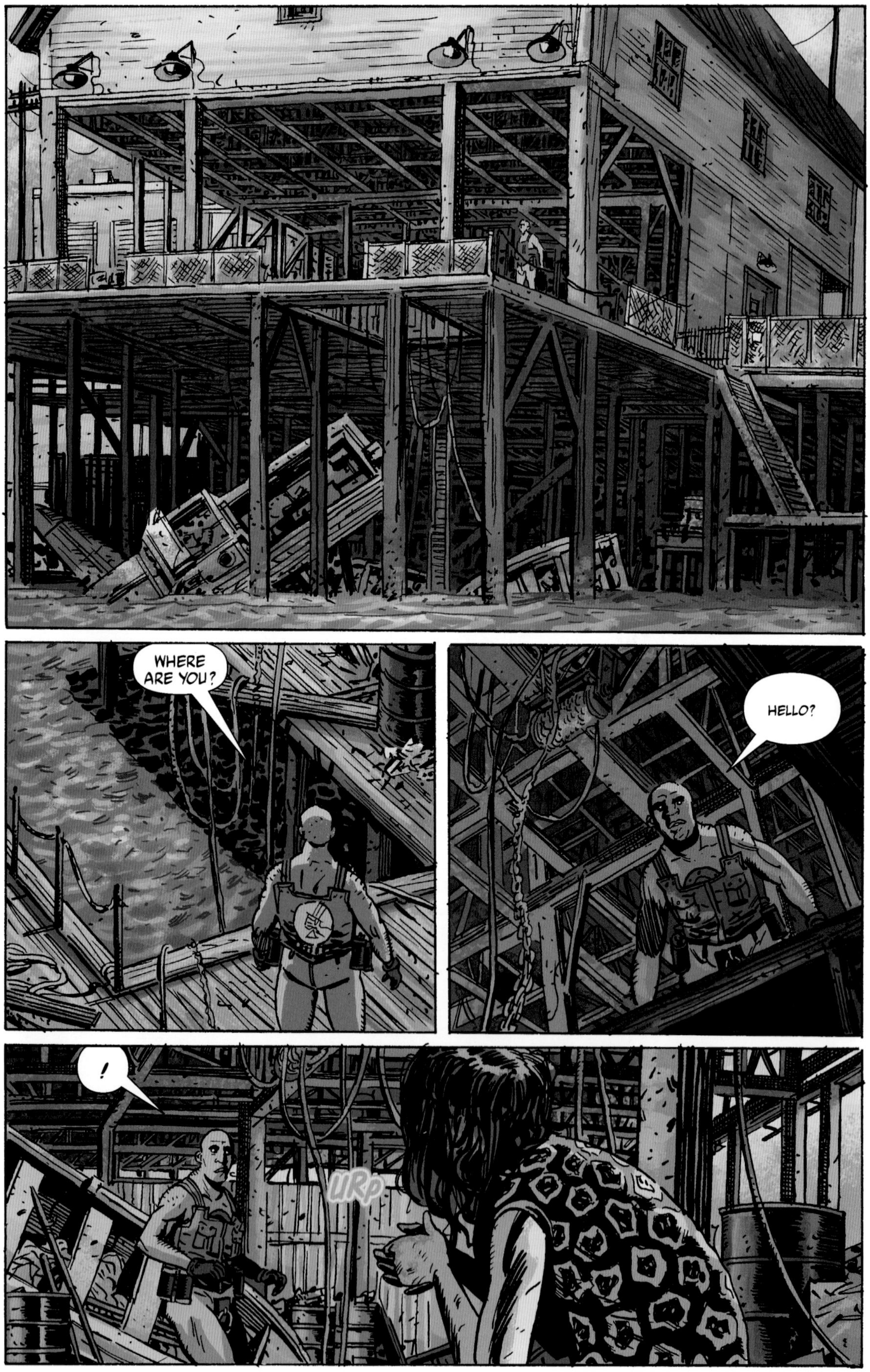

WHERE ARE YOU?
HELLO?
!
URP

LITTLE GIRL...?

·URRRP

URRRP

URRRP

OH!

RIBBIP

OH, I THOUGHT THAT...BUT YOU'RE ALL RIGHT.

DON'T BE AFRAID.

WHERE ARE YOUR PARENTS?

~~~~~~
~~~~
~~~~~

WHAT?

THE BLESSING OF THE LORD IS UPON ME.

HE HAS MADE ME HIS MESSENGER.

HE SAYS GO OUT AMONG HIS PEOPLE...

NO!

"AND GATHER THEM UNTO ME."

UROOONK

WHERE IS THE CHILD?

WHERE IS THE--

URNK URNK

SWOK

URRRNK

UGH!

URNK URNK

EVIL THING!

URNK

MAKE YOUR NOISE. YOU CANNOT--

"PLEASE..."

HELP ME.

YOU...

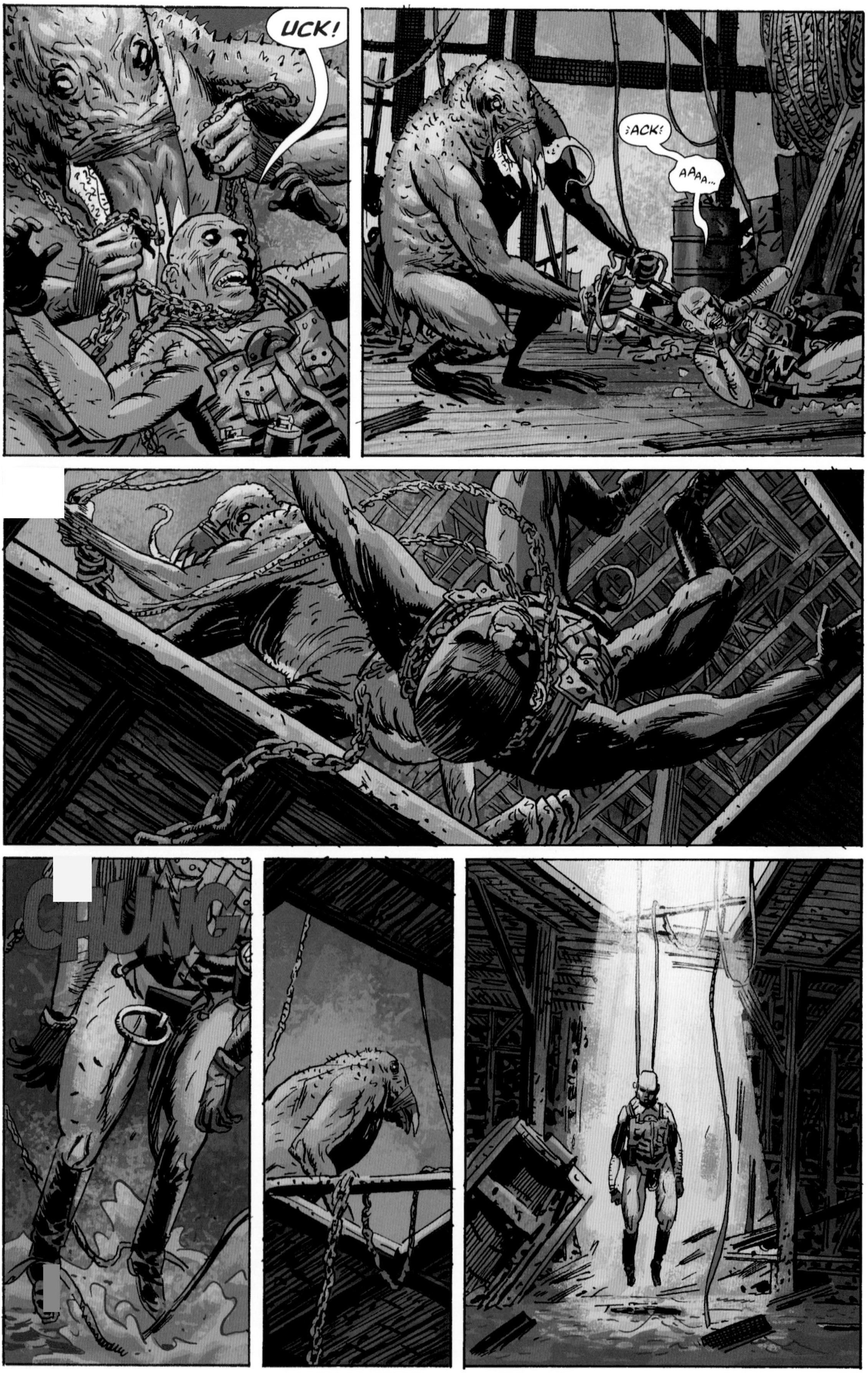
UCK!
ACK!
AAAA...
CHUNG

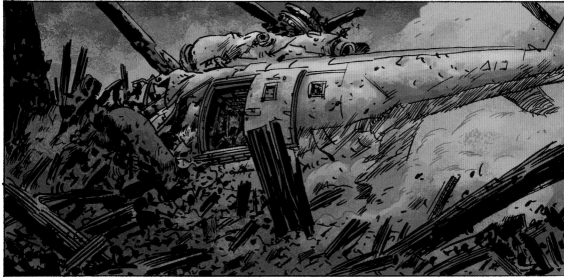

"ABRAHAM SAPIEN...

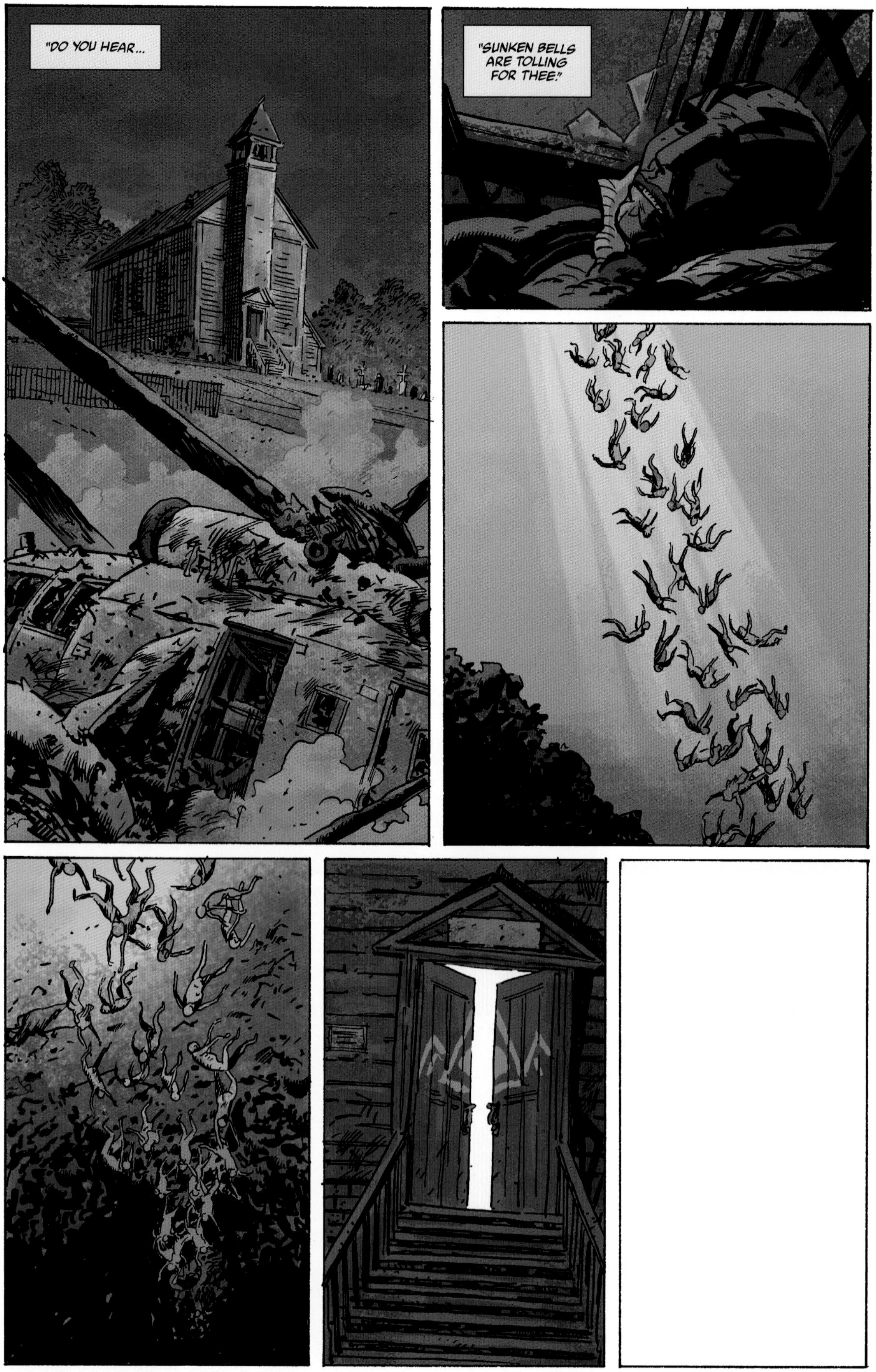
"DO YOU HEAR...
"SUNKEN BELLS ARE TOLLING FOR THEE."

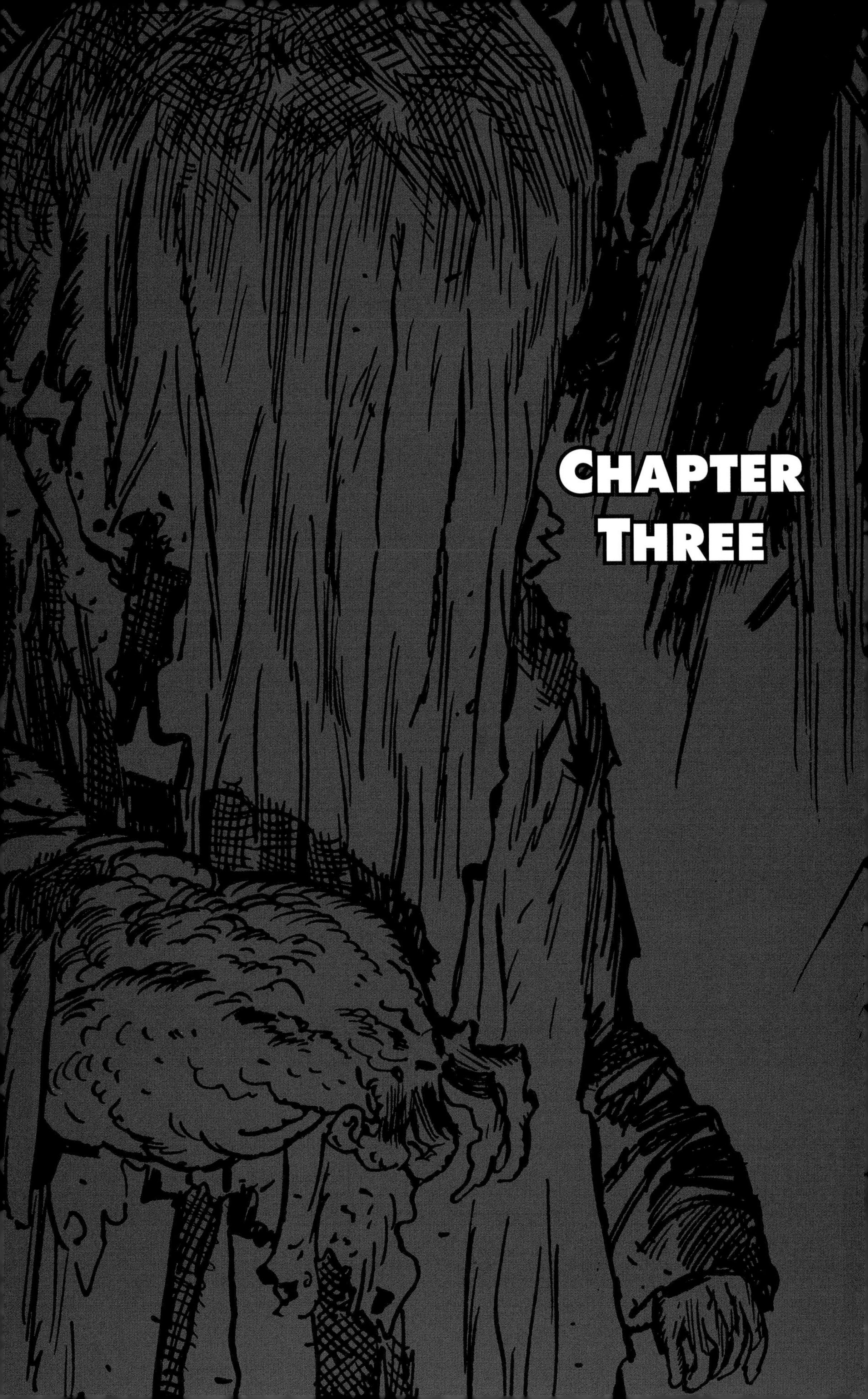
CHAPTER THREE

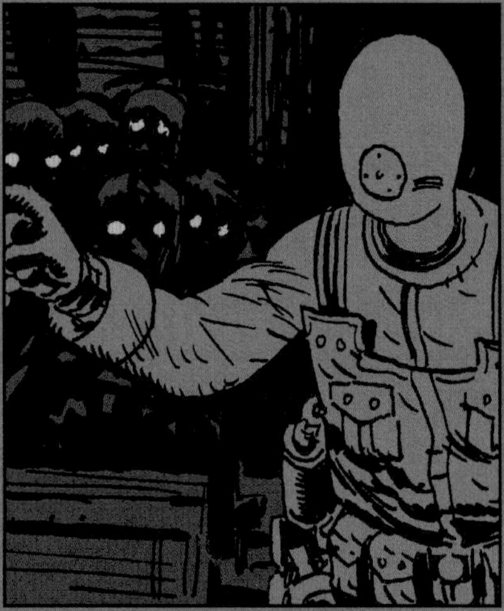

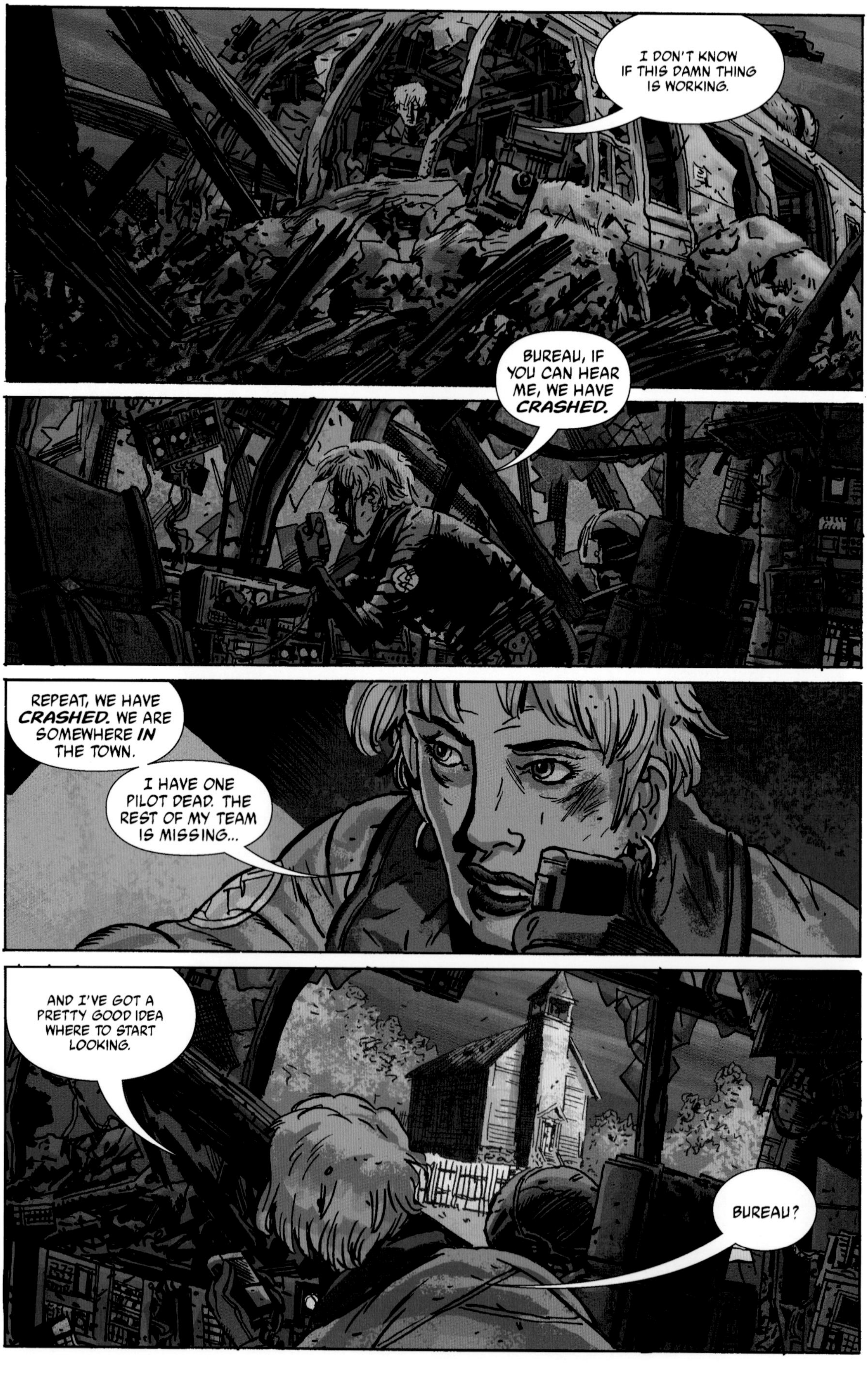
I DON'T KNOW IF THIS DAMN THING IS WORKING.
BUREAU, IF YOU CAN HEAR ME, WE HAVE *CRASHED.*
REPEAT, WE HAVE *CRASHED.* WE ARE SOMEWHERE *IN* THE TOWN.
I HAVE ONE PILOT DEAD. THE REST OF MY TEAM IS MISSING...
AND I'VE GOT A PRETTY GOOD IDEA WHERE TO START LOOKING.
BUREAU?

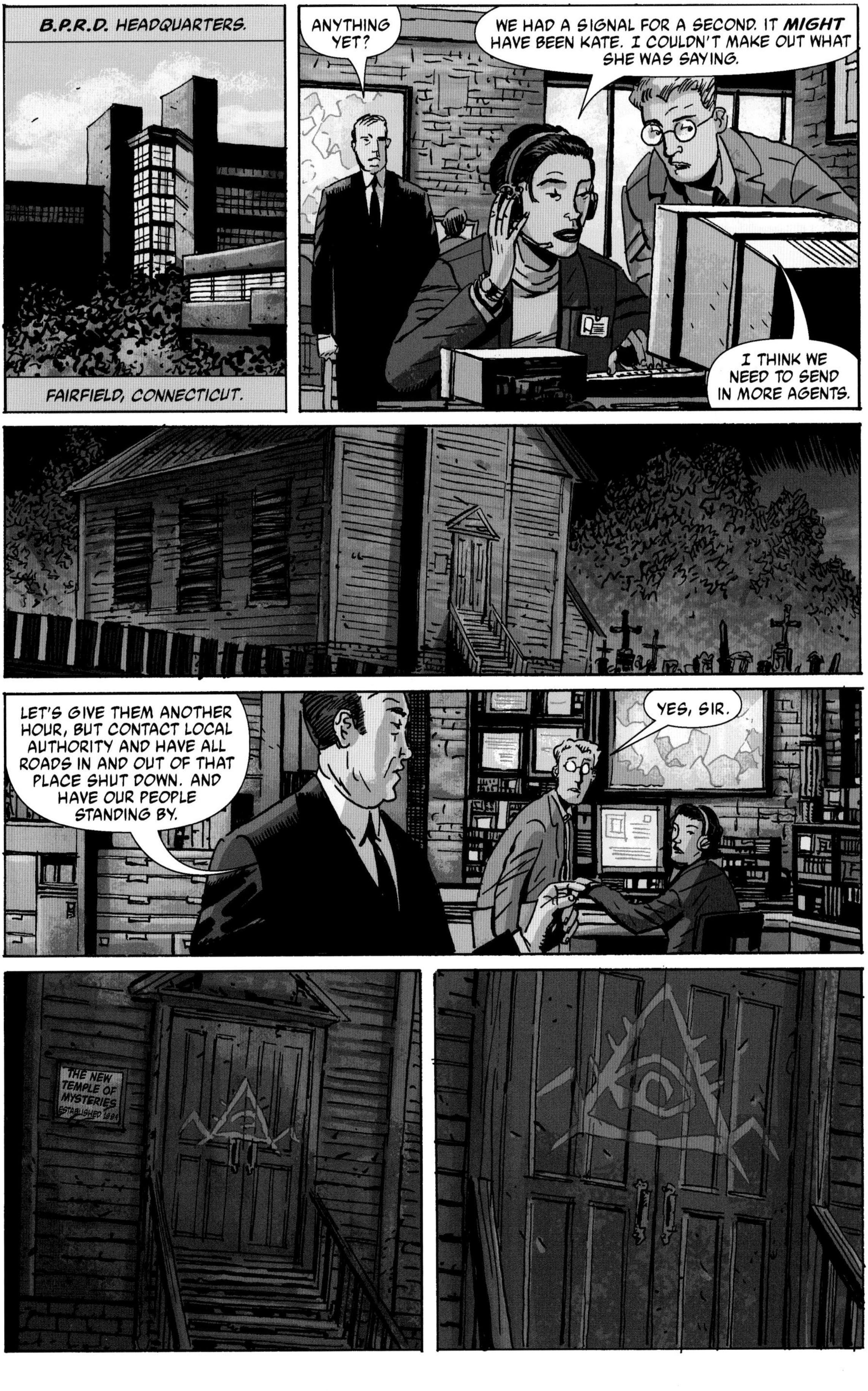
B.P.R.D. HEADQUARTERS.
FAIRFIELD, CONNECTICUT.
ANYTHING YET?
WE HAD A SIGNAL FOR A SECOND. IT MIGHT HAVE BEEN KATE. I COULDN'T MAKE OUT WHAT SHE WAS SAYING.
I THINK WE NEED TO SEND IN MORE AGENTS.
LET'S GIVE THEM ANOTHER HOUR, BUT CONTACT LOCAL AUTHORITY AND HAVE ALL ROADS IN AND OUT OF THAT PLACE SHUT DOWN. AND HAVE OUR PEOPLE STANDING BY.
YES, SIR.
THE NEW TEMPLE OF MYSTERIES ESTABLISHED 1994

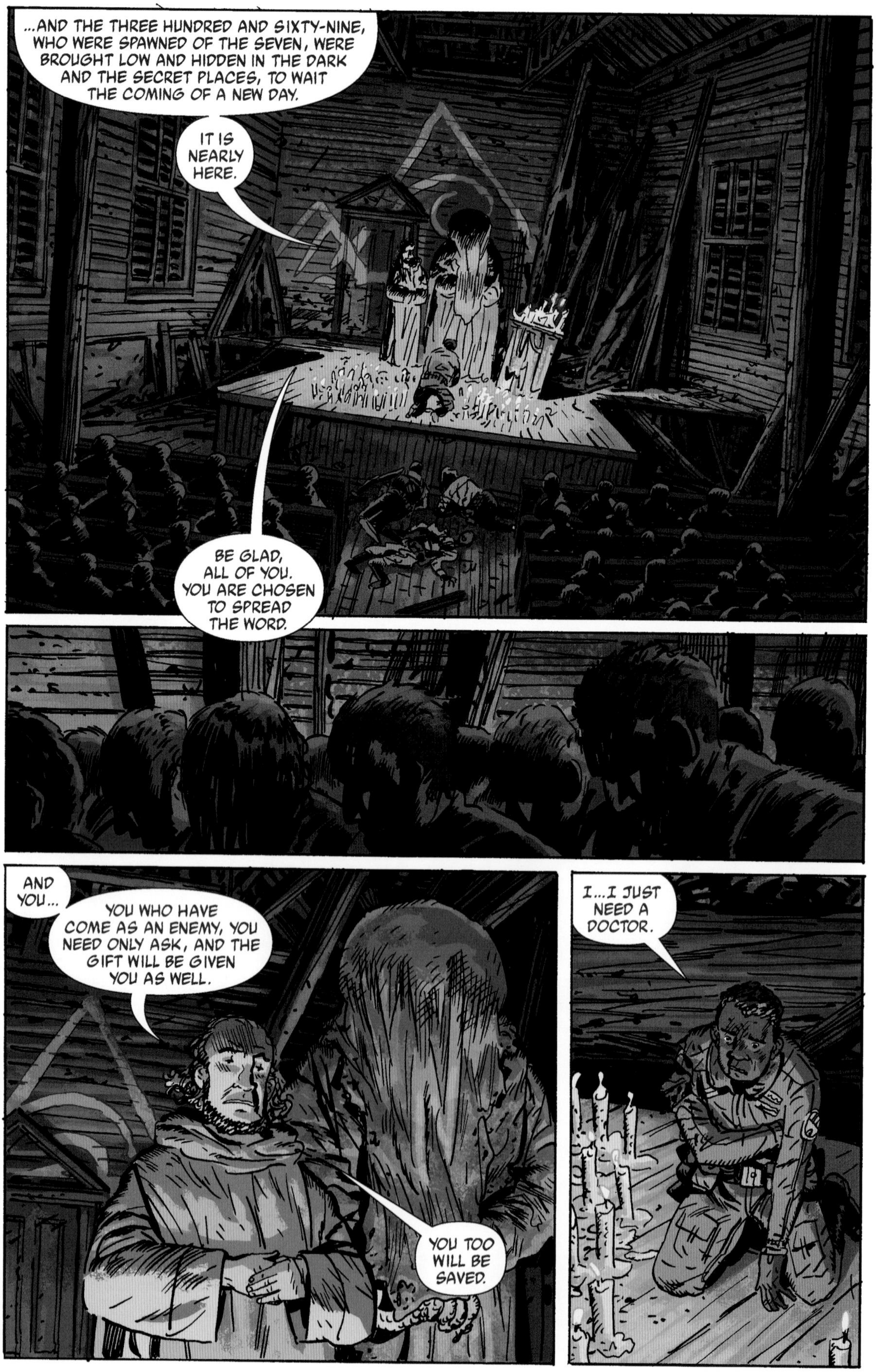
...AND THE THREE HUNDRED AND SIXTY-NINE, WHO WERE SPAWNED OF THE SEVEN, WERE BROUGHT LOW AND HIDDEN IN THE DARK AND THE SECRET PLACES, TO WAIT THE COMING OF A NEW DAY.
IT IS NEARLY HERE.
BE GLAD, ALL OF YOU. YOU ARE CHOSEN TO SPREAD THE WORD.
AND YOU...
YOU WHO HAVE COME AS AN ENEMY, YOU NEED ONLY ASK, AND THE GIFT WILL BE GIVEN YOU AS WELL.
YOU TOO WILL BE SAVED.
I...I JUST NEED A DOCTOR.

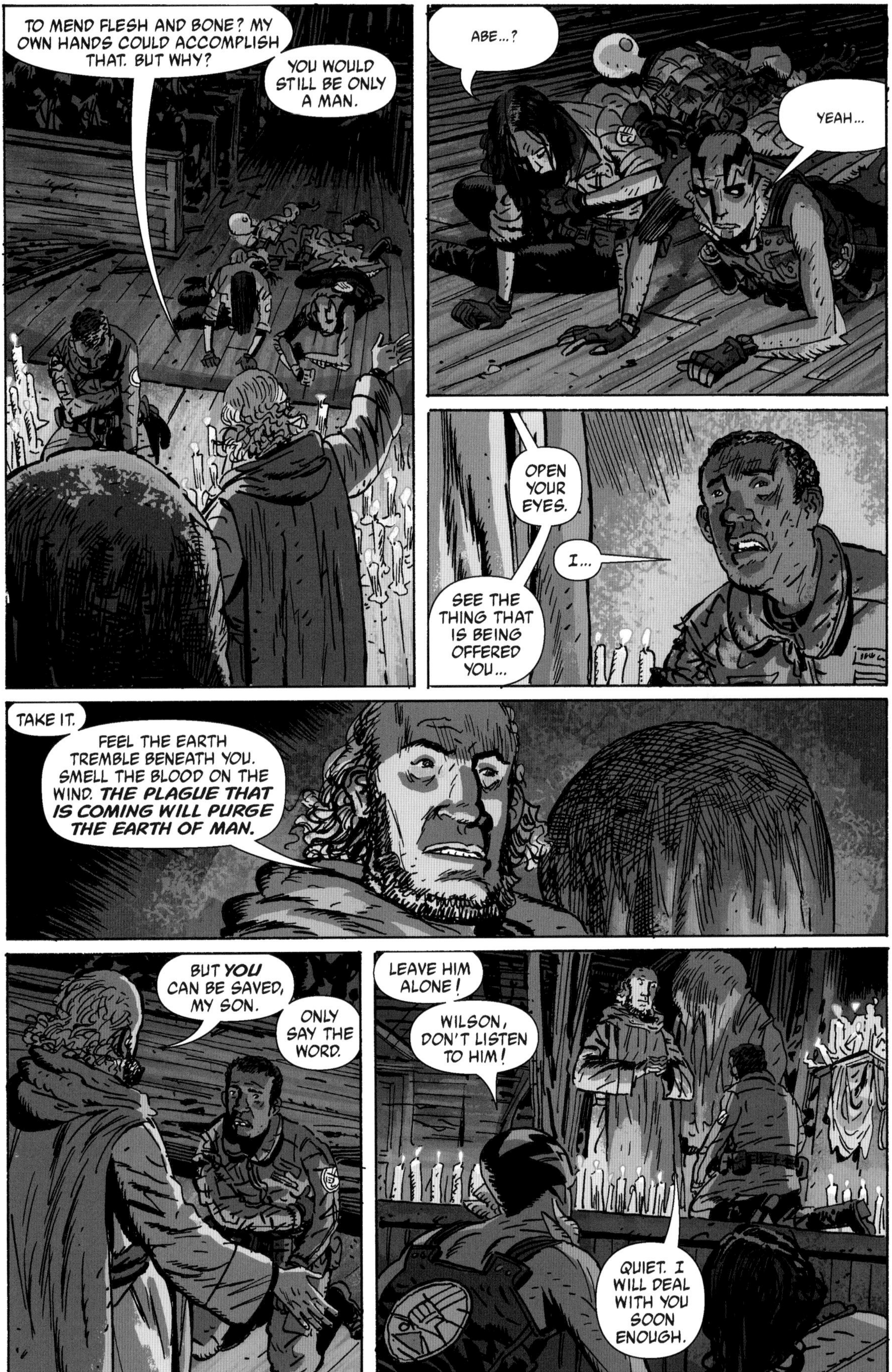
TO MEND FLESH AND BONE? MY OWN HANDS COULD ACCOMPLISH THAT. BUT WHY?
YOU WOULD STILL BE ONLY A MAN.
ABE...?
YEAH...
OPEN YOUR EYES.
I...
SEE THE THING THAT IS BEING OFFERED YOU...
TAKE IT.
FEEL THE EARTH TREMBLE BENEATH YOU. SMELL THE BLOOD ON THE WIND. THE PLAGUE THAT IS COMING WILL PURGE THE EARTH OF MAN.
BUT YOU CAN BE SAVED, MY SON.
ONLY SAY THE WORD.
LEAVE HIM ALONE!
WILSON, DON'T LISTEN TO HIM!
QUIET. I WILL DEAL WITH YOU SOON ENOUGH.

BEHOLD.

ETH EM-ED SADU-HEM. SPAWNED OF THE DRAGON AND RISEN FROM HIS OWN GRAVE, AND COME UNTO US TO PREPARE THE WAY...

IT DOESN'T MATTER THAT YOU CANNOT SPEAK. HE SEES WHAT IS WRITTEN IN YOUR HEART.

HE HAS CHOSEN YOU.

...

I...

I'M TRYING, BUT... I CAN'T...

LIZ...!

POK

SON OF A...

RURP

RURRP

"REJOICE. HE IS SAVED."

RURP

UUM-EMM BLU AG DISH.

RURP

MY SON, RECEIVE THE GOOD NEWS. THE GODS ARE COMING.

WAHNSINNIGER! YOU HAVE GIVEN YOURSELF OVER TO EVIL POWERS...

RURP

AH, THE TALKING BAG.

IN THIS LIFE, OR THE NEXT, YOUR SOUL WILL PAY!

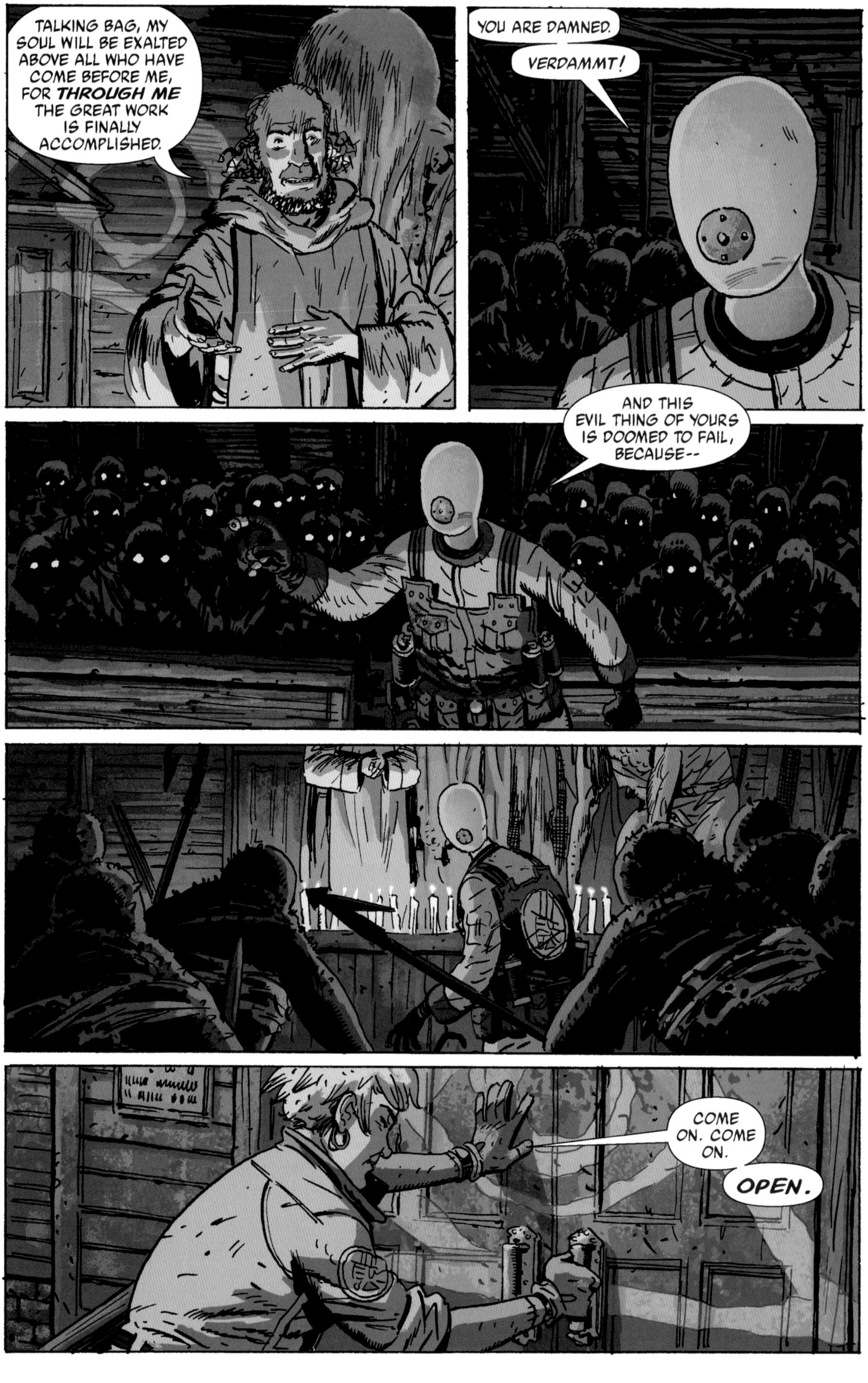
TALKING BAG, MY SOUL WILL BE EXALTED ABOVE ALL WHO HAVE COME BEFORE ME, FOR **THROUGH ME** THE GREAT WORK IS FINALLY ACCOMPLISHED.
YOU ARE DAMNED.
VERDAMMT!
AND THIS EVIL THING OF YOURS IS DOOMED TO FAIL, BECAUSE--
COME ON. COME ON.
OPEN.

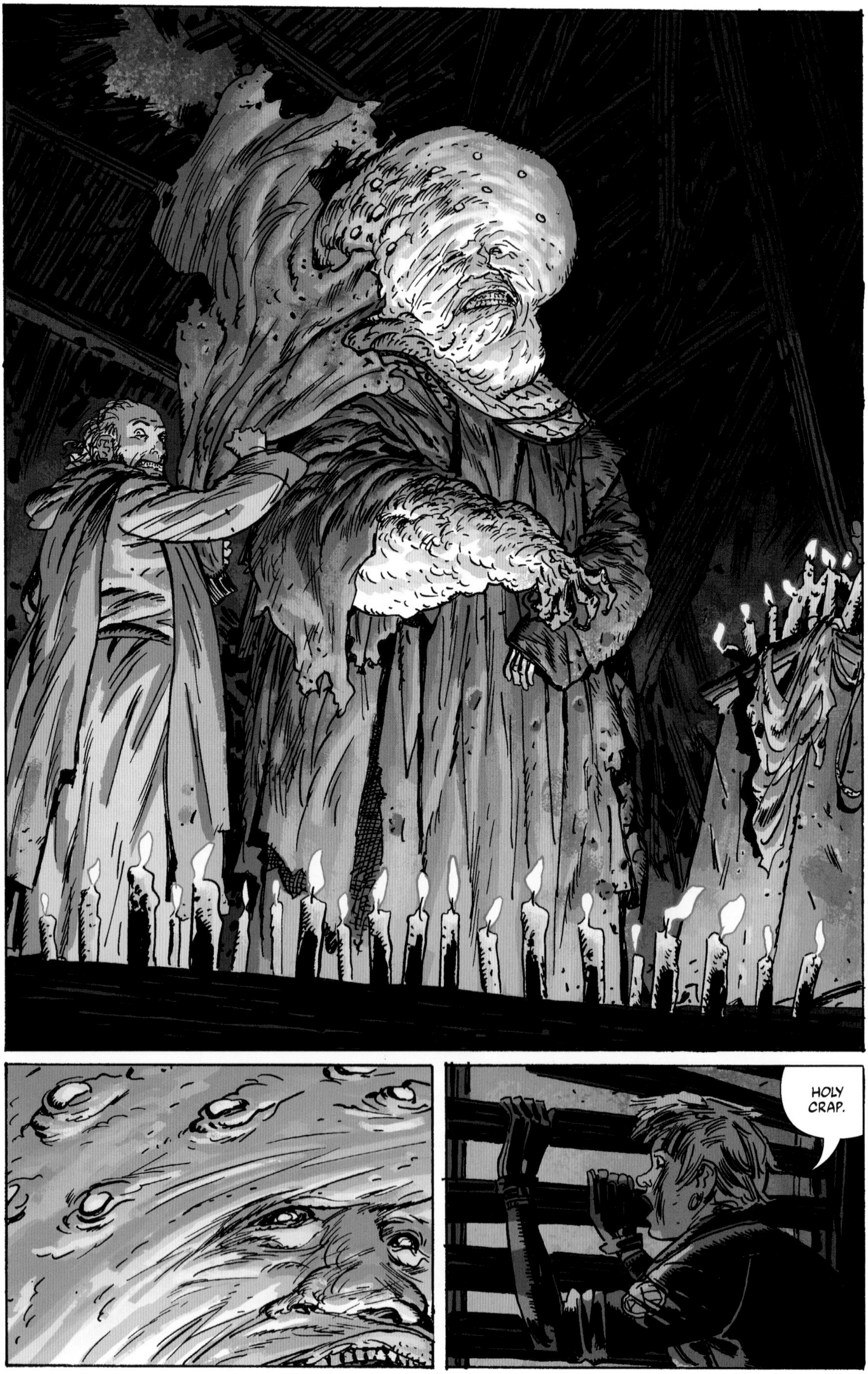
HOLY CRAP.

IBISHHH SHUGAAAAAAA...

EM ETH OGDRU JEHAD. OGDRU SADU-HEM ET.

DAMN IT!

LIZ...

I'M TRYING, ABE... I'M TRYING...

SOMETHING ABOUT THIS PLACE...CAN'T CONCENTRATE...

YOU CAN DO IT.

CAN'T CONCENTRATE...

"THE FIRE IS NOT MY ENEMY...

"IT IS A PART OF ME...

"IT IS MINE."

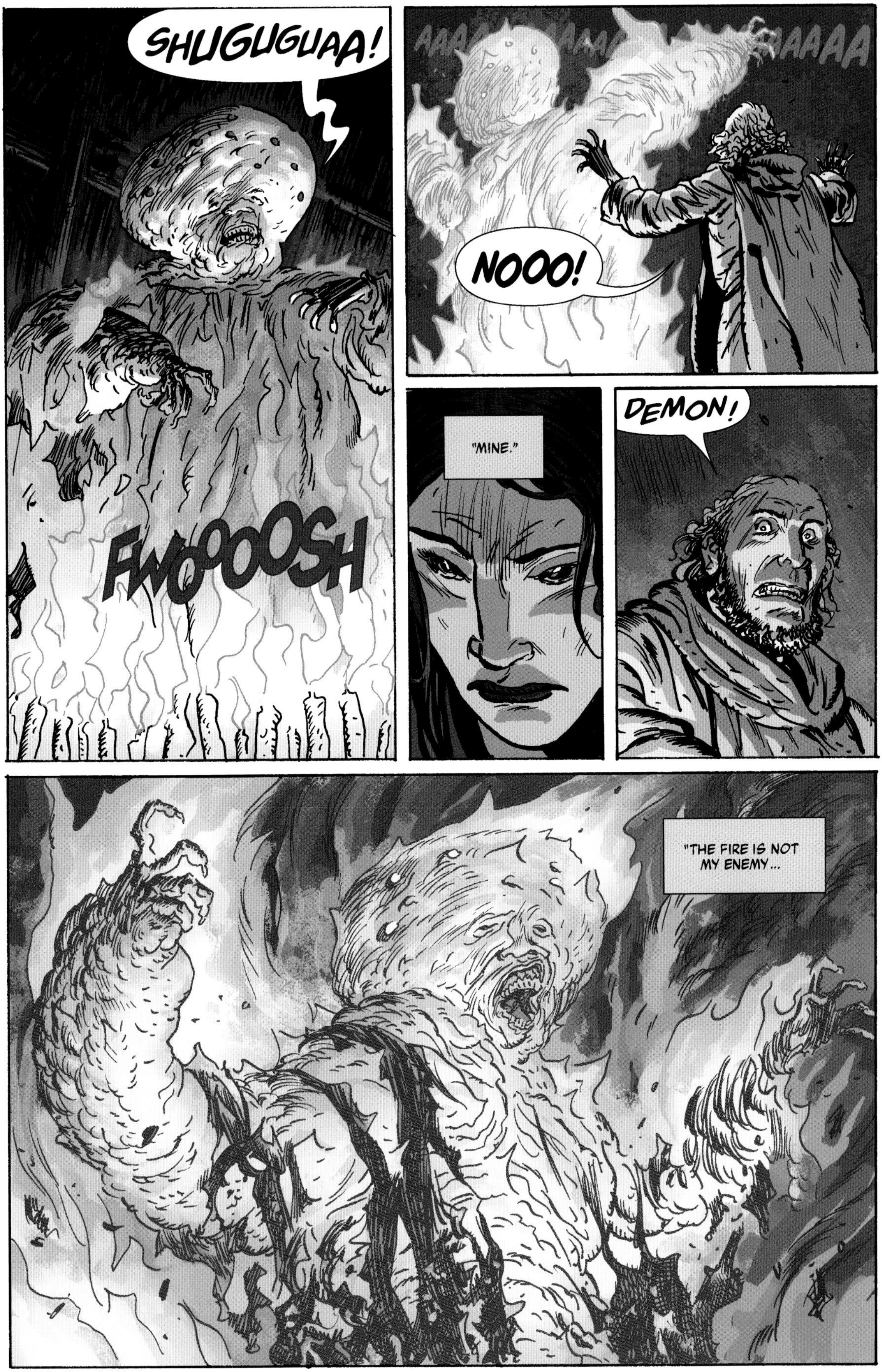
SHUGUGUAA!
FWOOOOSH
AAAAAAAAAAAAAA
NOOO!
"MINE."
DEMON!
"THE FIRE IS NOT MY ENEMY...

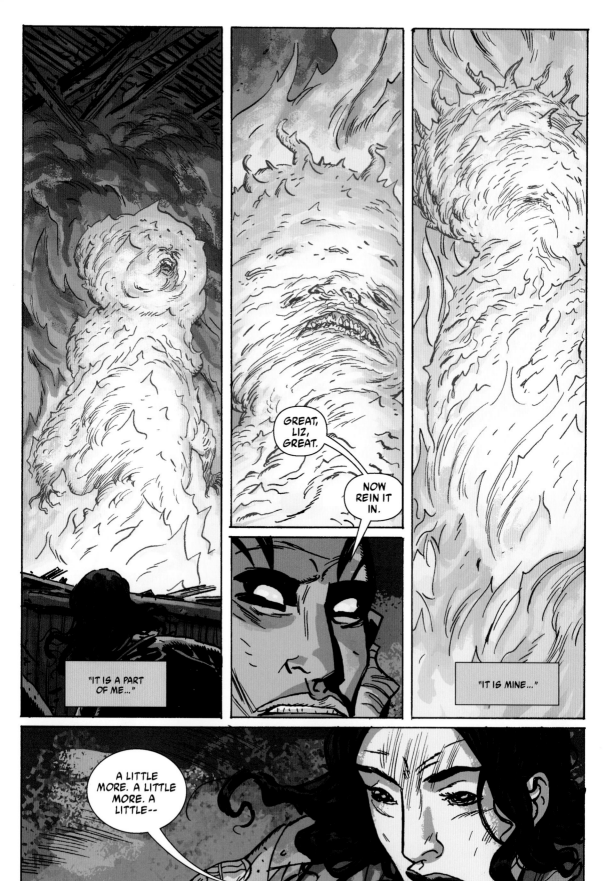

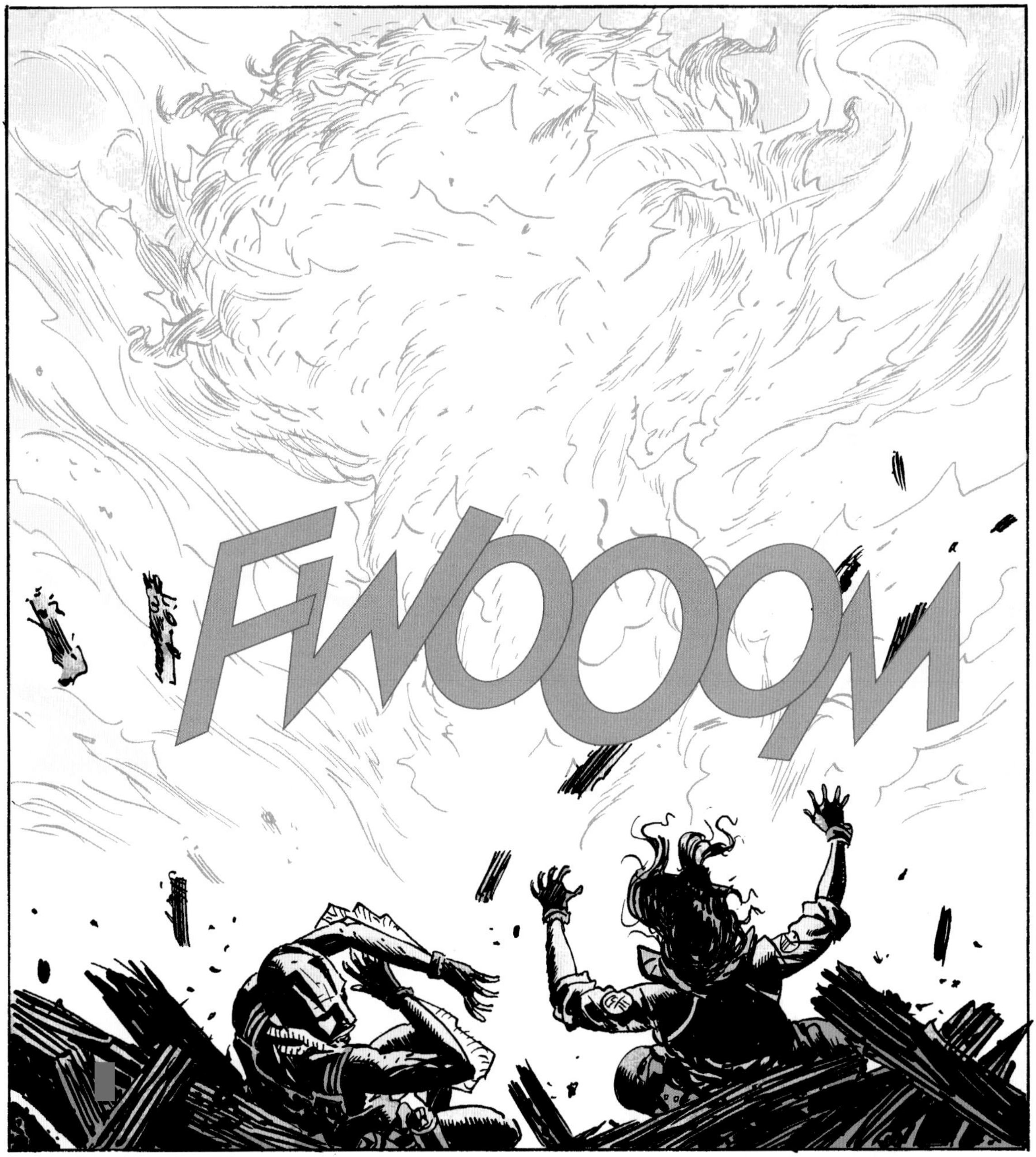
FWOOOM

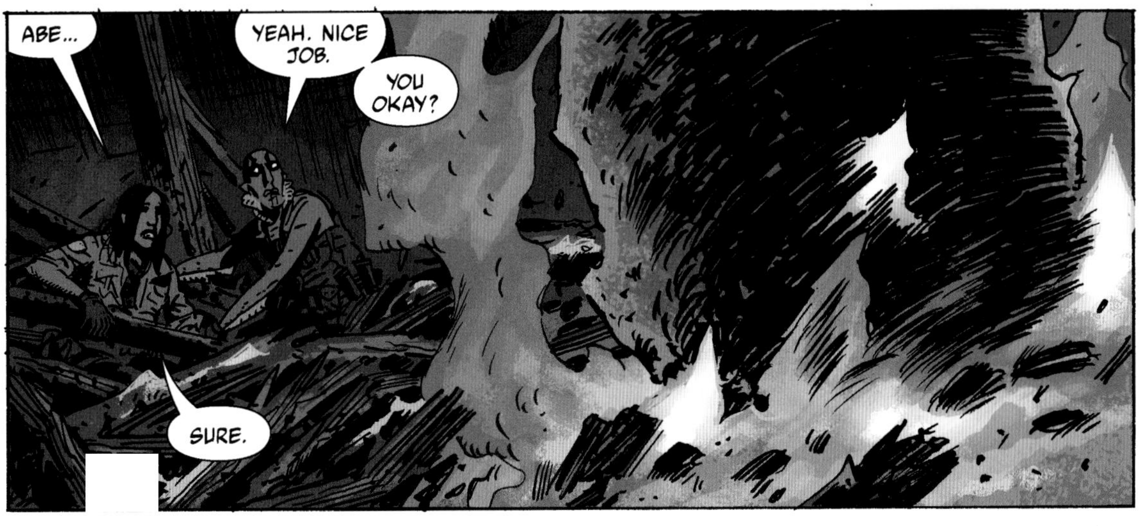
ABE...
YEAH. NICE JOB.
YOU OKAY?
SURE.

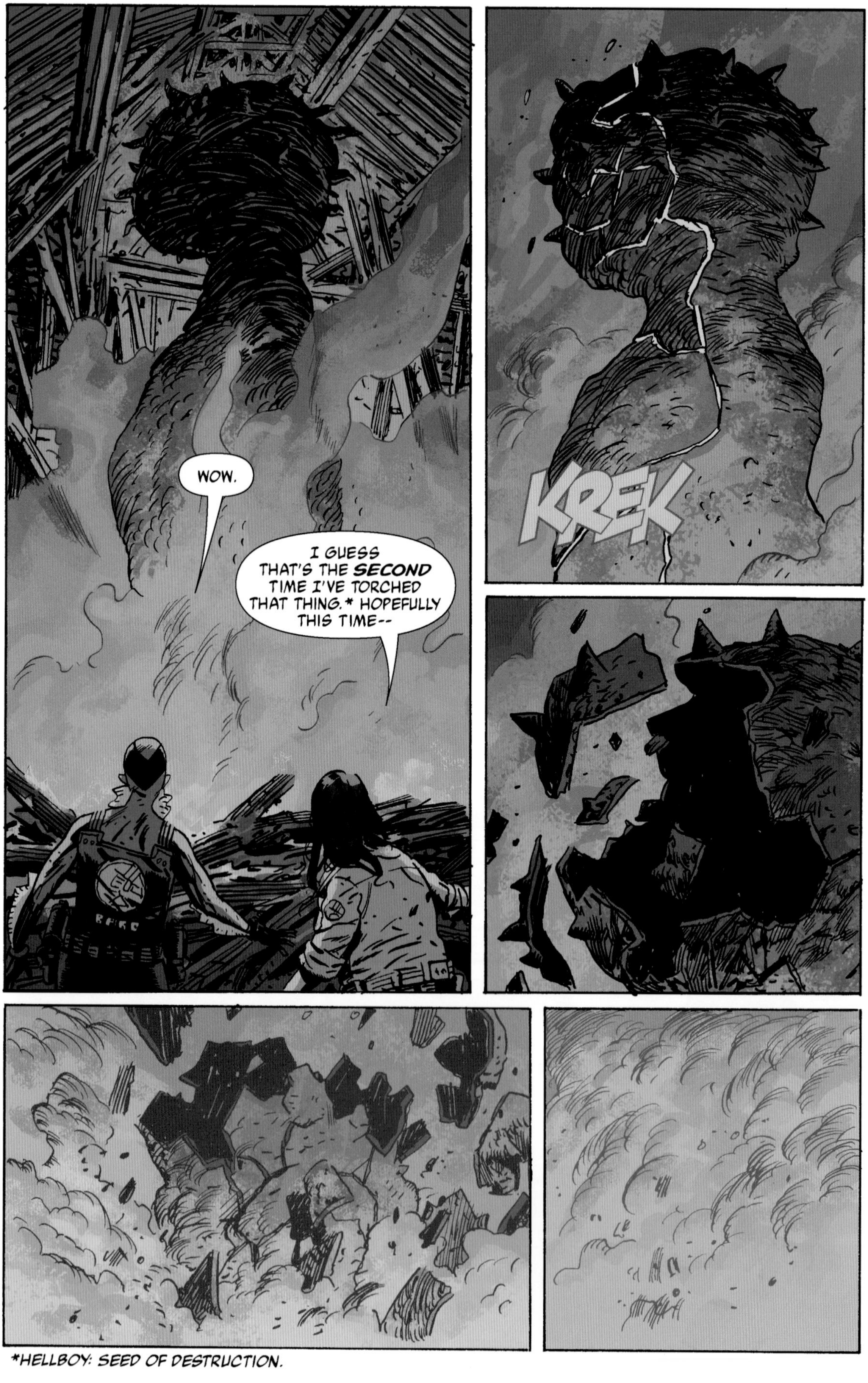
WOW.
I GUESS THAT'S THE **SECOND** TIME I'VE TORCHED THAT THING.* HOPEFULLY THIS TIME--
KREK

*HELLBOY: SEED OF DESTRUCTION.

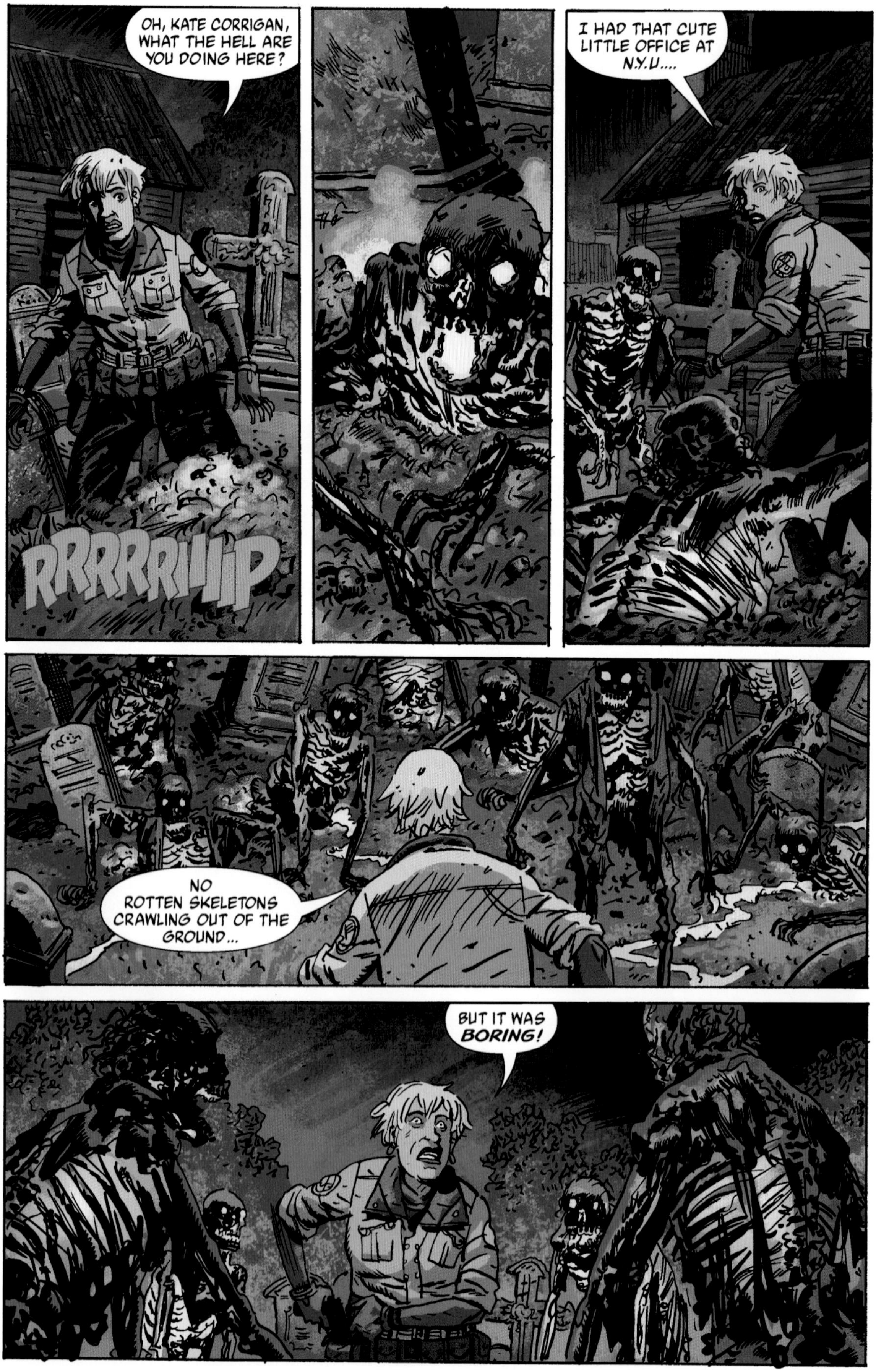
OH, KATE CORRIGAN, WHAT THE HELL ARE YOU DOING HERE?
RRRRRIIIIP
I HAD THAT CUTE LITTLE OFFICE AT N.Y.U....
NO ROTTEN SKELETONS CRAWLING OUT OF THE GROUND...
BUT IT WAS *BORING!*

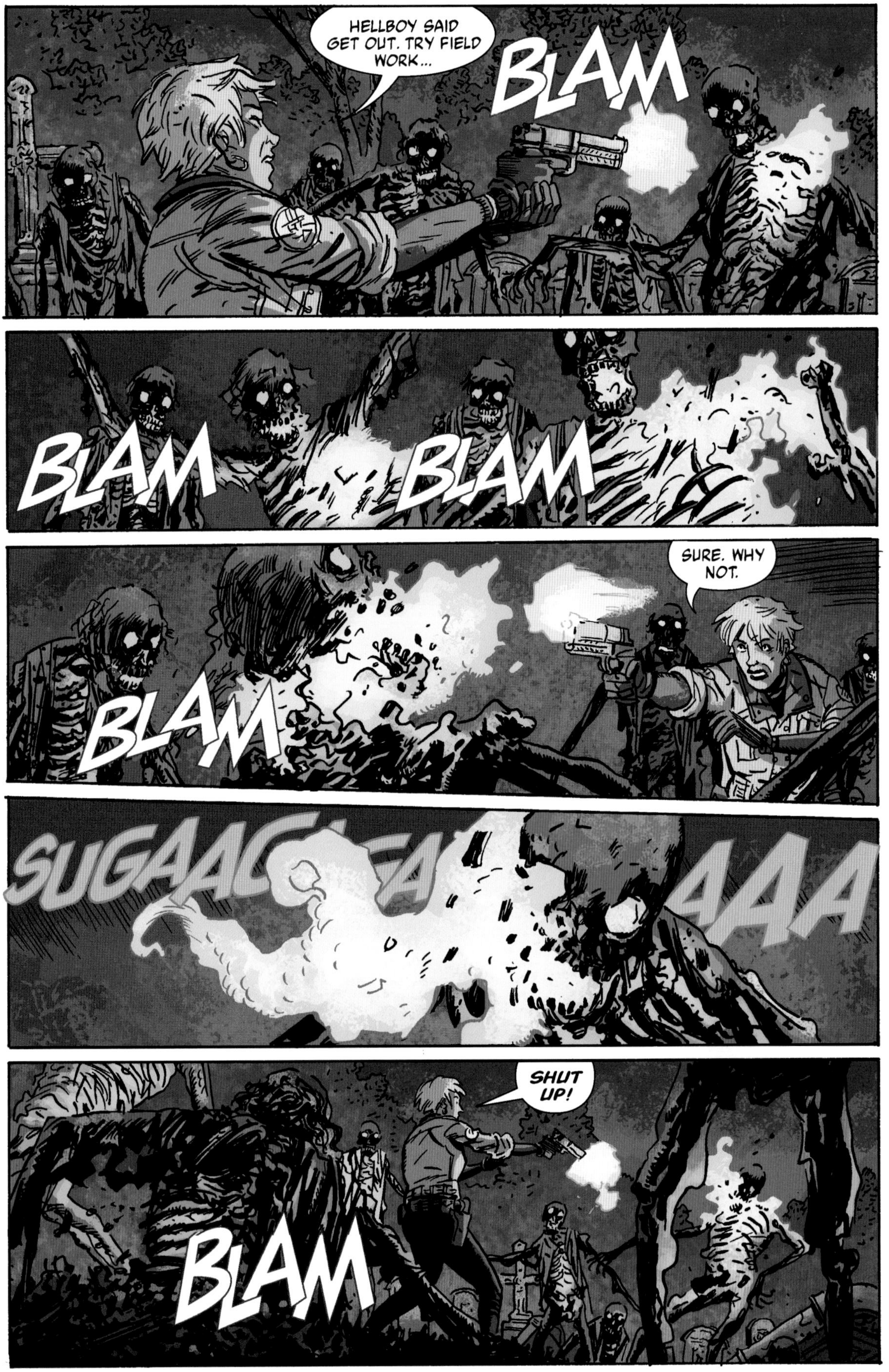
HELLBOY SAID GET OUT. TRY FIELD WORK...
BLAM
BLAM
BLAM
SURE. WHY NOT.
BLAM
SUGAAC
AAA
SHUT UP!
BLAM

GUN SHOTS?

KATE.

BLAM

I'LL GET HER.

YOU GO AFTER THE NUT IN THE ROBE.

BLAM

BLAM

URP

URP

URP

CREEEEK

RUUURp

CLICK

CHAPTER
FOUR

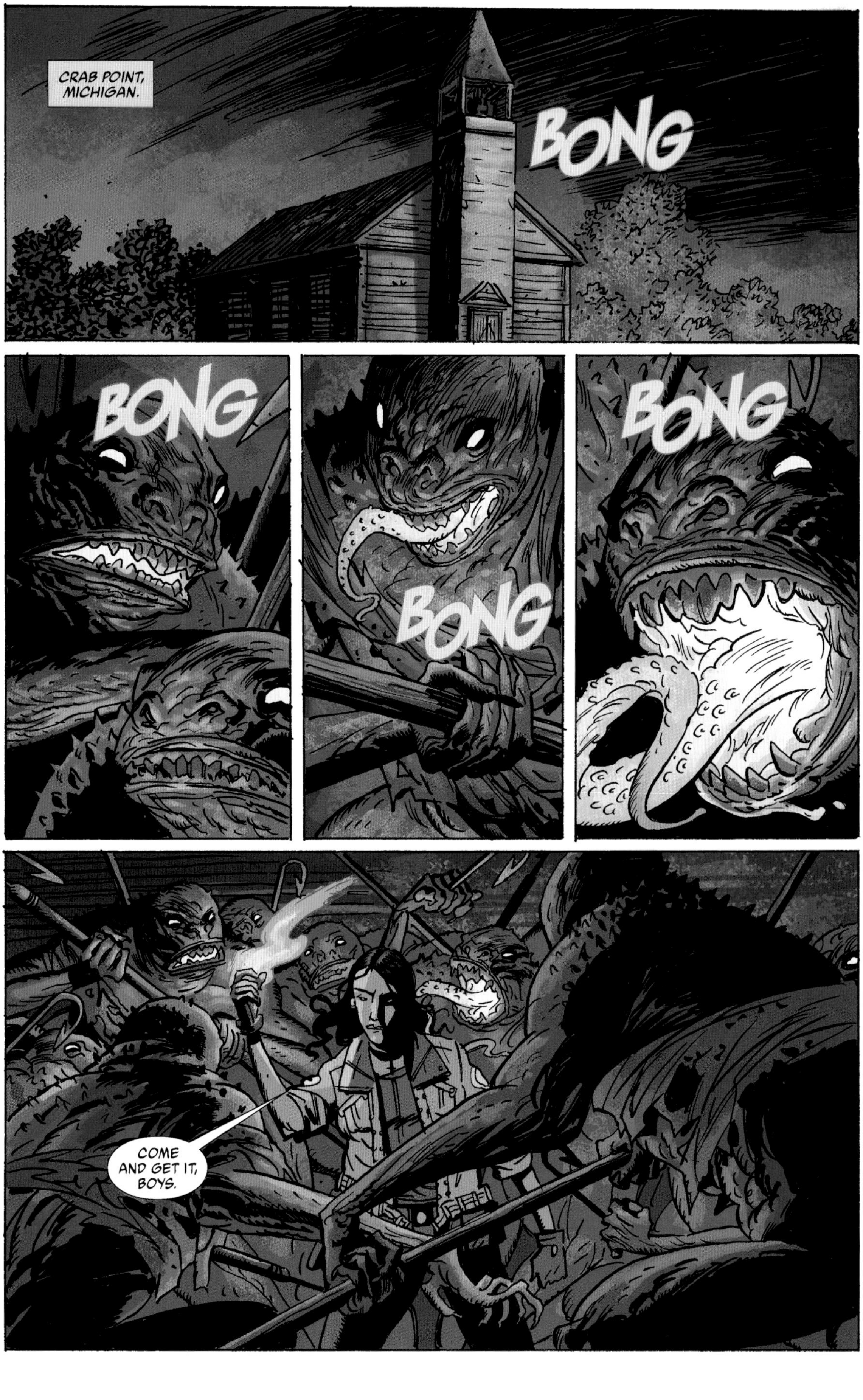
CRAB POINT, MICHIGAN.
BONG
BONG
BONG
BONG
COME AND GET IT, BOYS.

FWOOOOOOOOOOOOM

URRRAARAARR

RARP
RAARP
RARP
RARP

"THE FIRE IS NOT MY ENEMY...

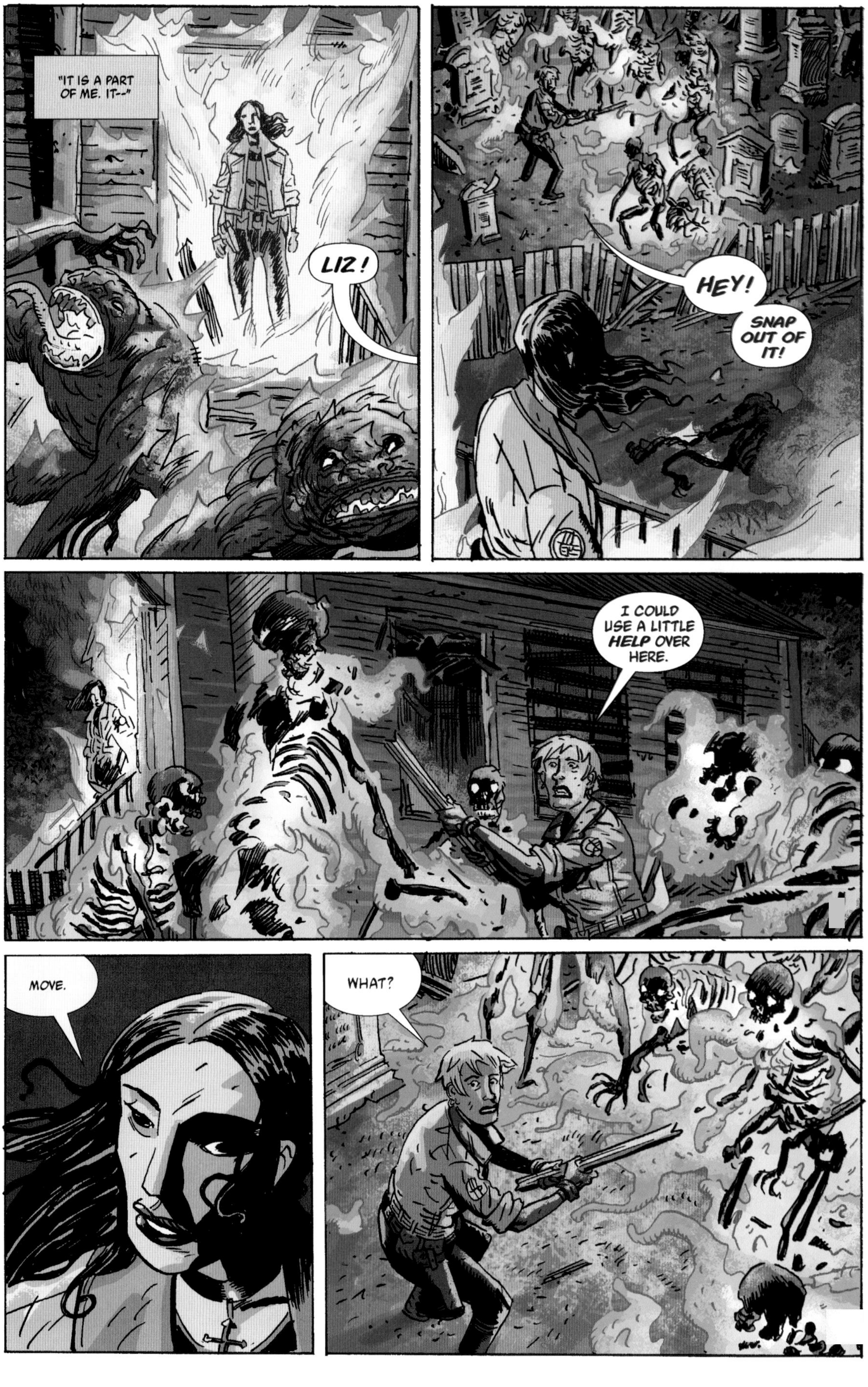
"IT IS A PART OF ME. IT--"
LIZ!
HEY!
SNAP OUT OF IT!
I COULD USE A LITTLE HELP OVER HERE.
MOVE.
WHAT?

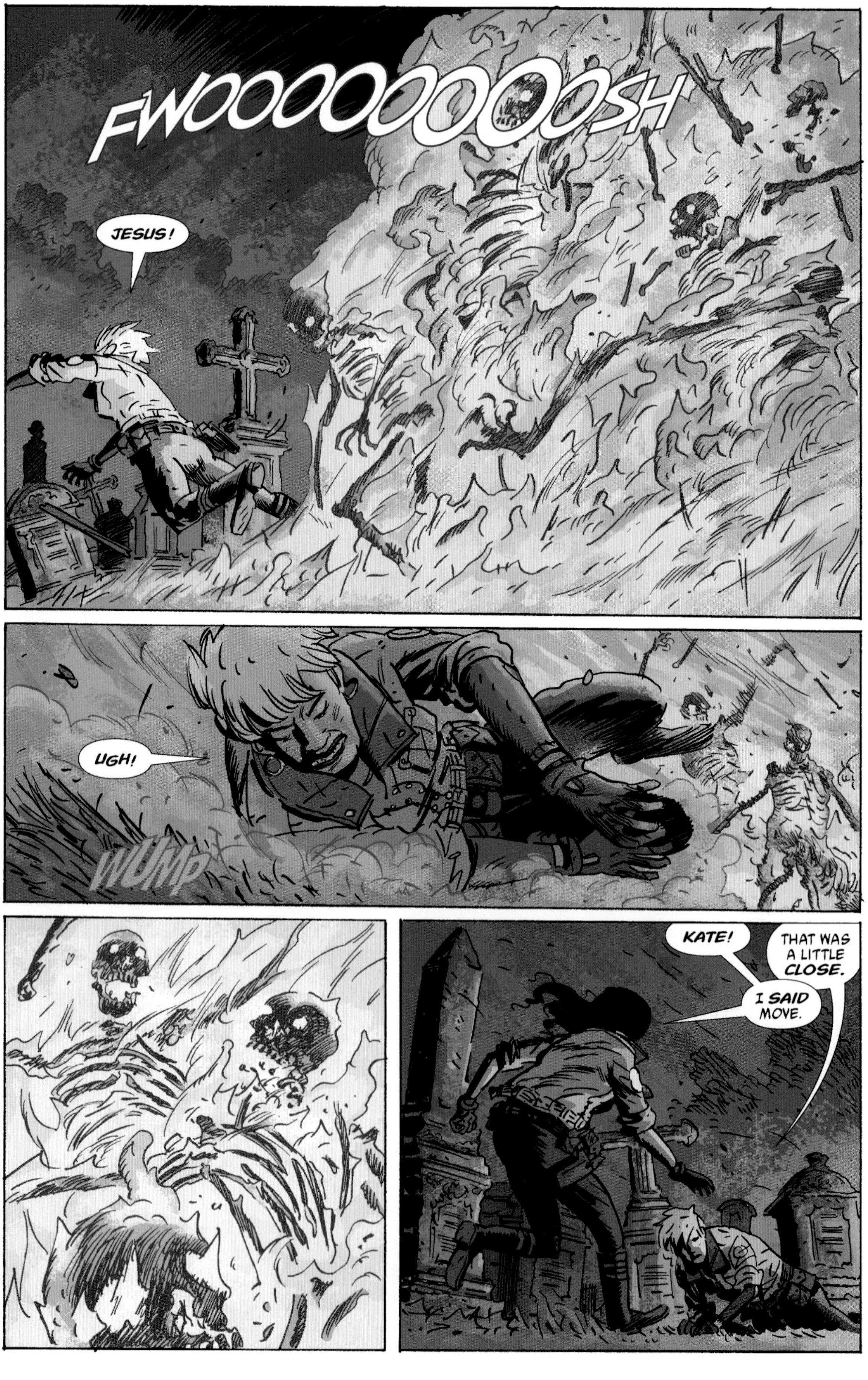
FWOOOOOOOOOSH
JESUS!
UGH!
WUMP
KATE!
I SAID MOVE.
THAT WAS A LITTLE CLOSE.

IT'S OKAY.

SO WHAT DID I MISS?

DOCTOR-WHAT'S-HIS-NAME APPARENTLY TURNED INTO A GIANT ELEPHANT-MAN FUNGUS GUY, AND HE'S MIXED UP WITH A CRAZY DOOMSDAY-CULT PRIEST GUY...

AND BETWEEN THE TWO OF THEM IT LOOKS LIKE THEY TURNED THE WHOLE TOWN INTO FROG MONSTERS.

THE WHOLE TOWN...

JOHANN...?

I SAW THAT.

TORN UP BY THE FROG GUYS AND BLOWN OUT THE WINDOW BY THE PRIEST.

YEAH...

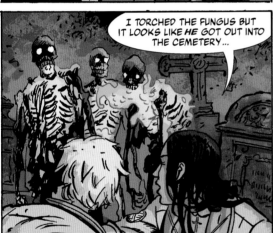

I TORCHED THE FUNGUS BUT IT LOOKS LIKE HE GOT OUT INTO THE CEMETERY...

NOT GOING TO BE A PROBLEM THOUGH...

"THE FIRE IS A PART OF ME..."

WOOOOOOSH

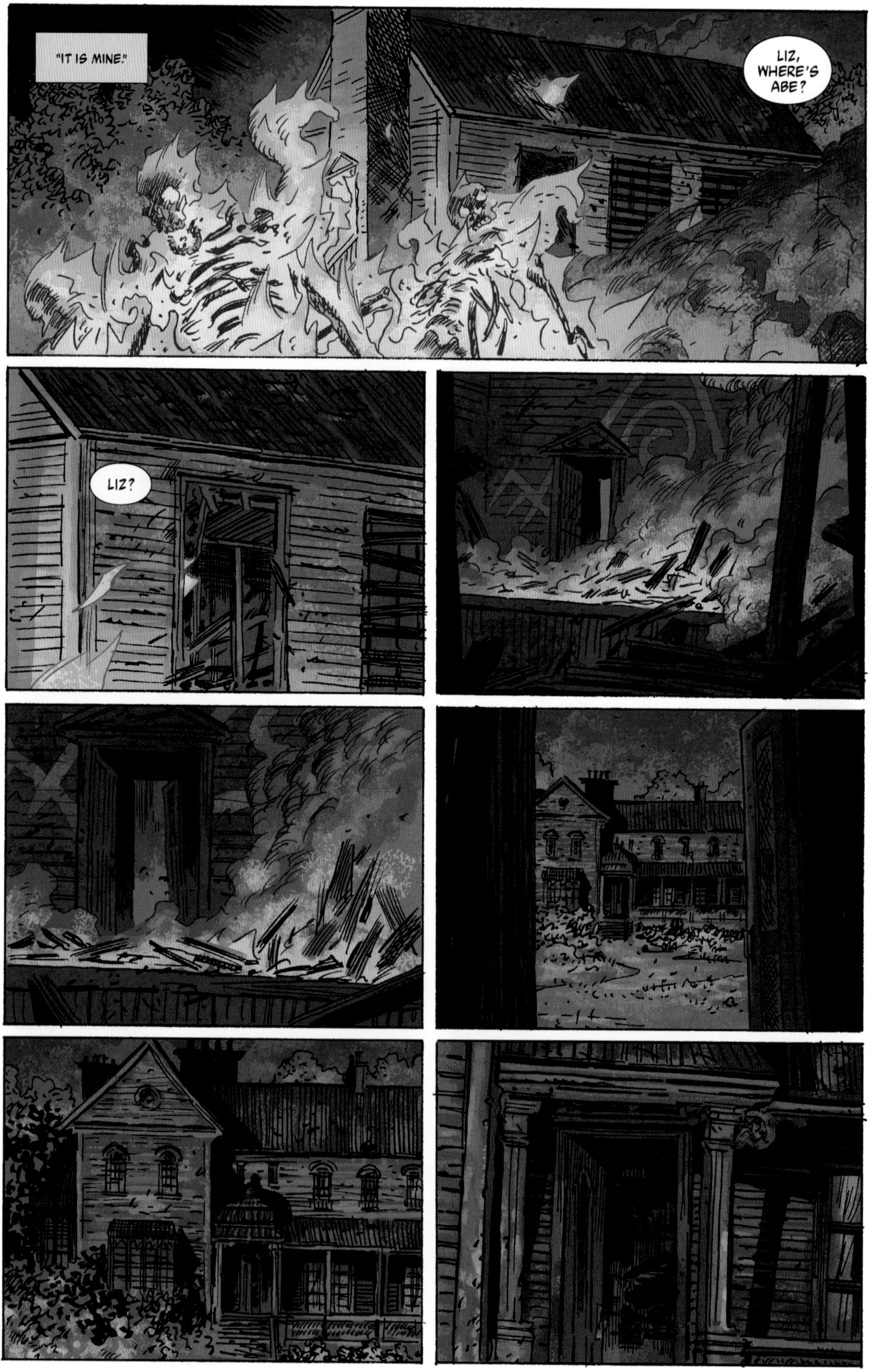
"IT IS MINE."
LIZ, WHERE'S ABE?
LIZ?

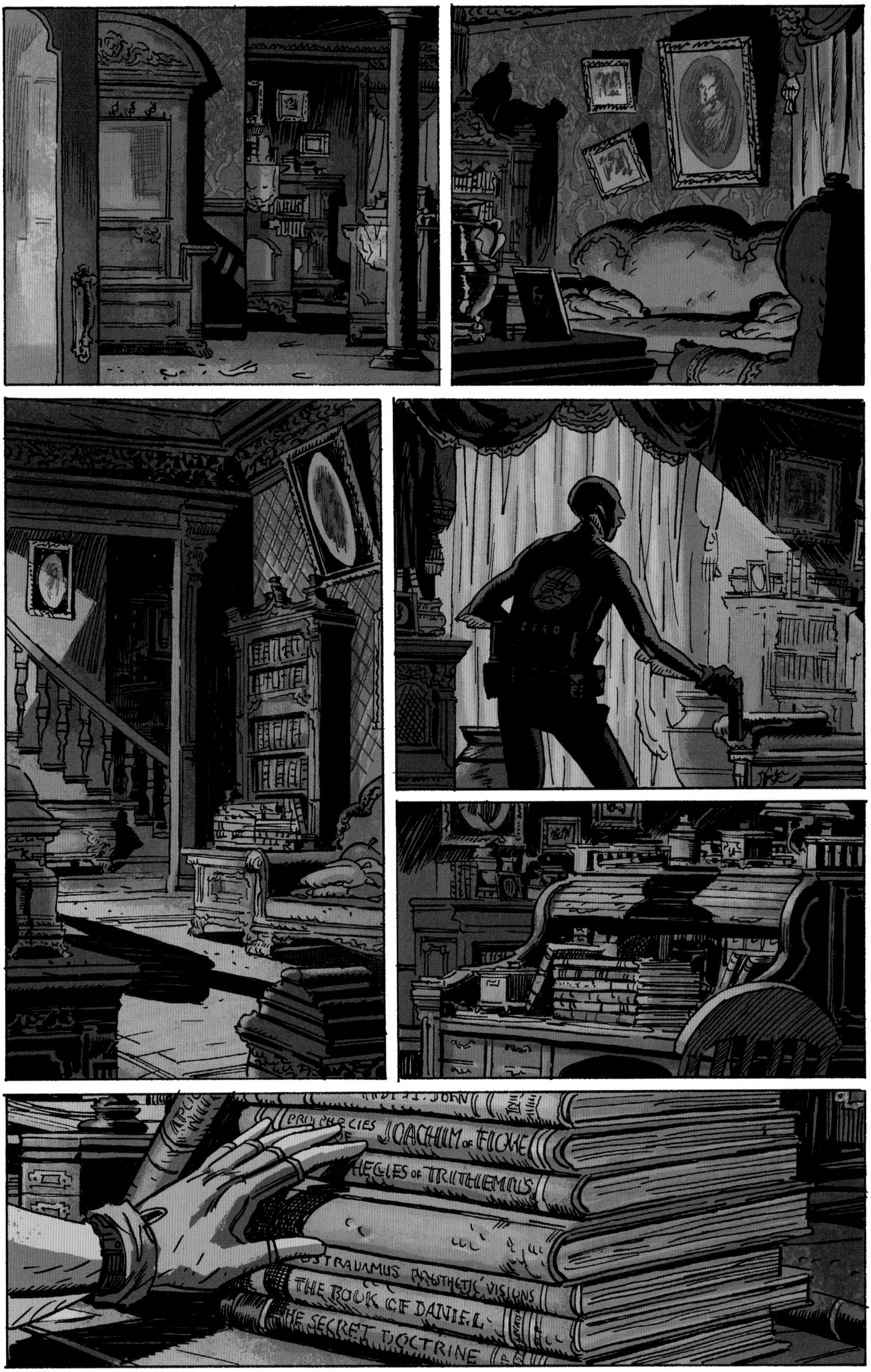
PROPHECIES
JOACHIM OF FIORE
HECIES OF TRITHEMIUS
THE BOOK OF DANIEL
THE SECRET DOCTRINE

?

SCRAPBOOK.

"NINE-YEAR-OLD HUMBERT T. JONES, OF MARNET, WEST VIRGINIA, APPARENTLY HEALED THE BROKEN ARM OF A CLASSMATE..."

"MIRACLE BOY"

DOZENS CLAIM CURED BY MIRACLE BOY

I WAS CURED BY WEST VIRGINIA MIRACLE BOY

"DOCTORS CONFIRM THAT TUMORS HAVE VANISHED..."

HEALING POWER BAFFLES EXPERTS

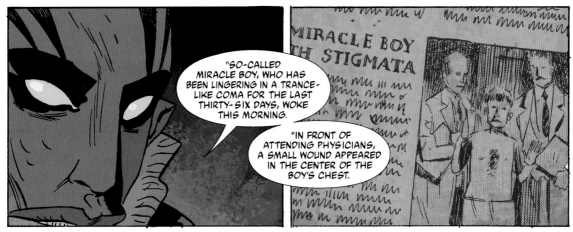

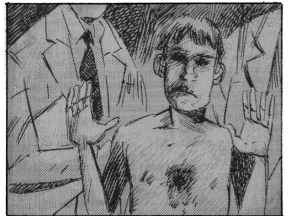

* CAVENDISH HALL WAS DESTROYED BY AN EXPLOSION ON MAY 11, 1994.

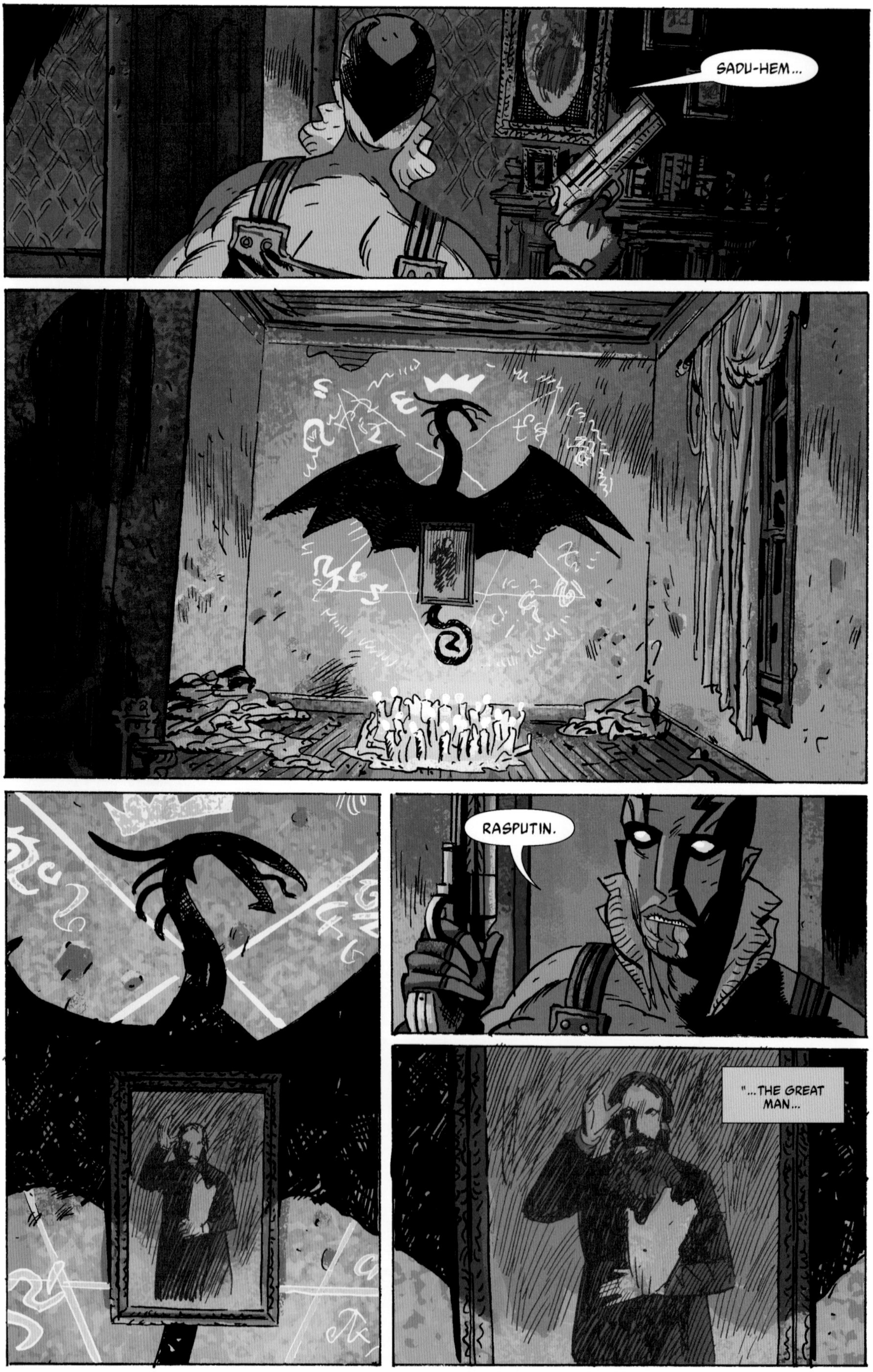
SADU-HEM...
RASPUTIN.
"...THE GREAT MAN...

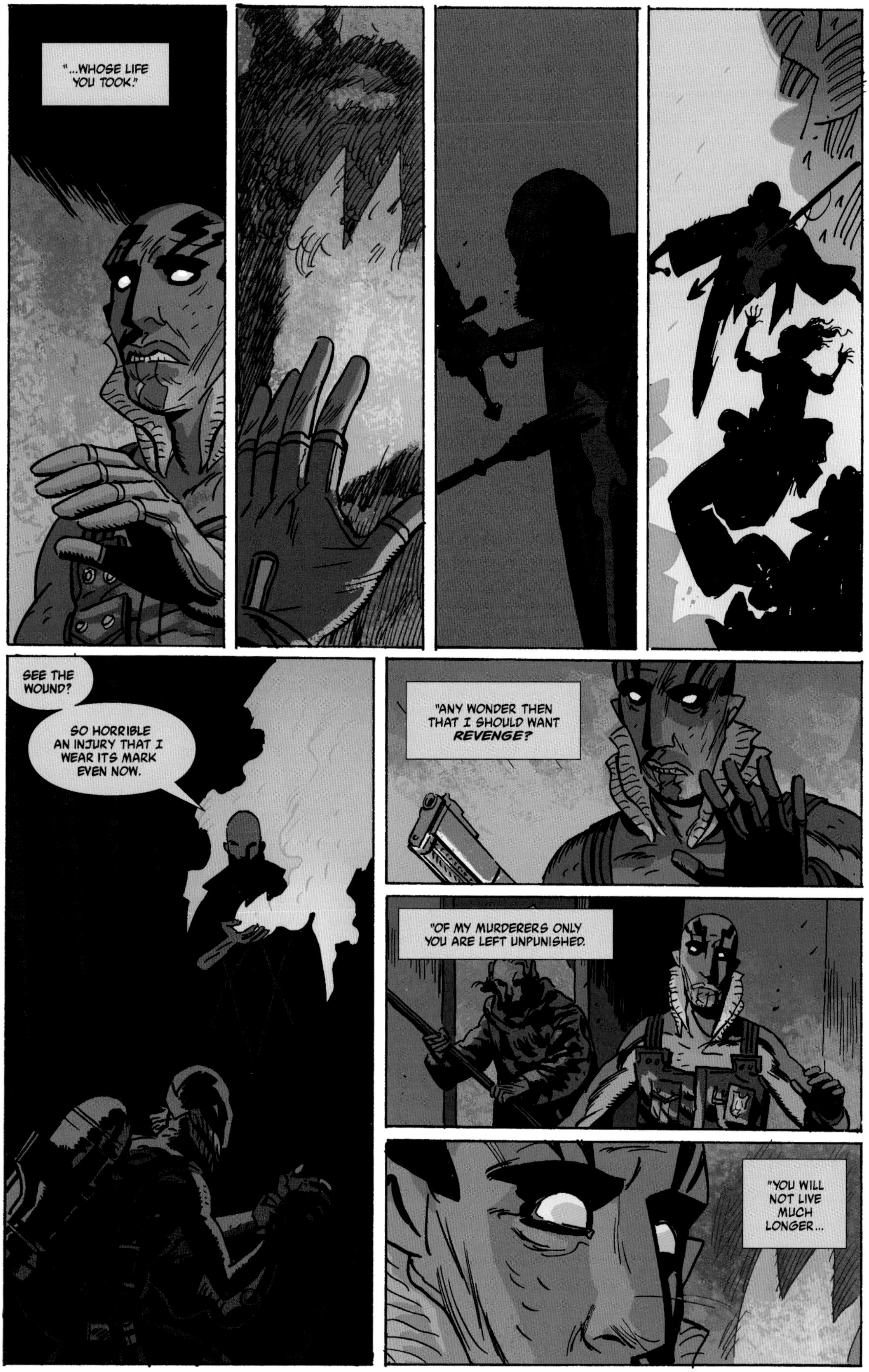
"...WHOSE LIFE YOU TOOK."
SEE THE WOUND?
SO HORRIBLE AN INJURY THAT I WEAR ITS MARK EVEN NOW.
"ANY WONDER THEN THAT I SHOULD WANT *REVENGE?*
"OF MY MURDERERS ONLY YOU ARE LEFT UNPUNISHED.
"YOU WILL NOT LIVE MUCH LONGER...

"YOU WILL DIE AS *I* DIED..."

BLAM

AHHH!

"AND THE HANDS ON THE SPEAR SHAFT WILL BELONG TO ANOTHER..."

BLAM

BLAM

BLAM

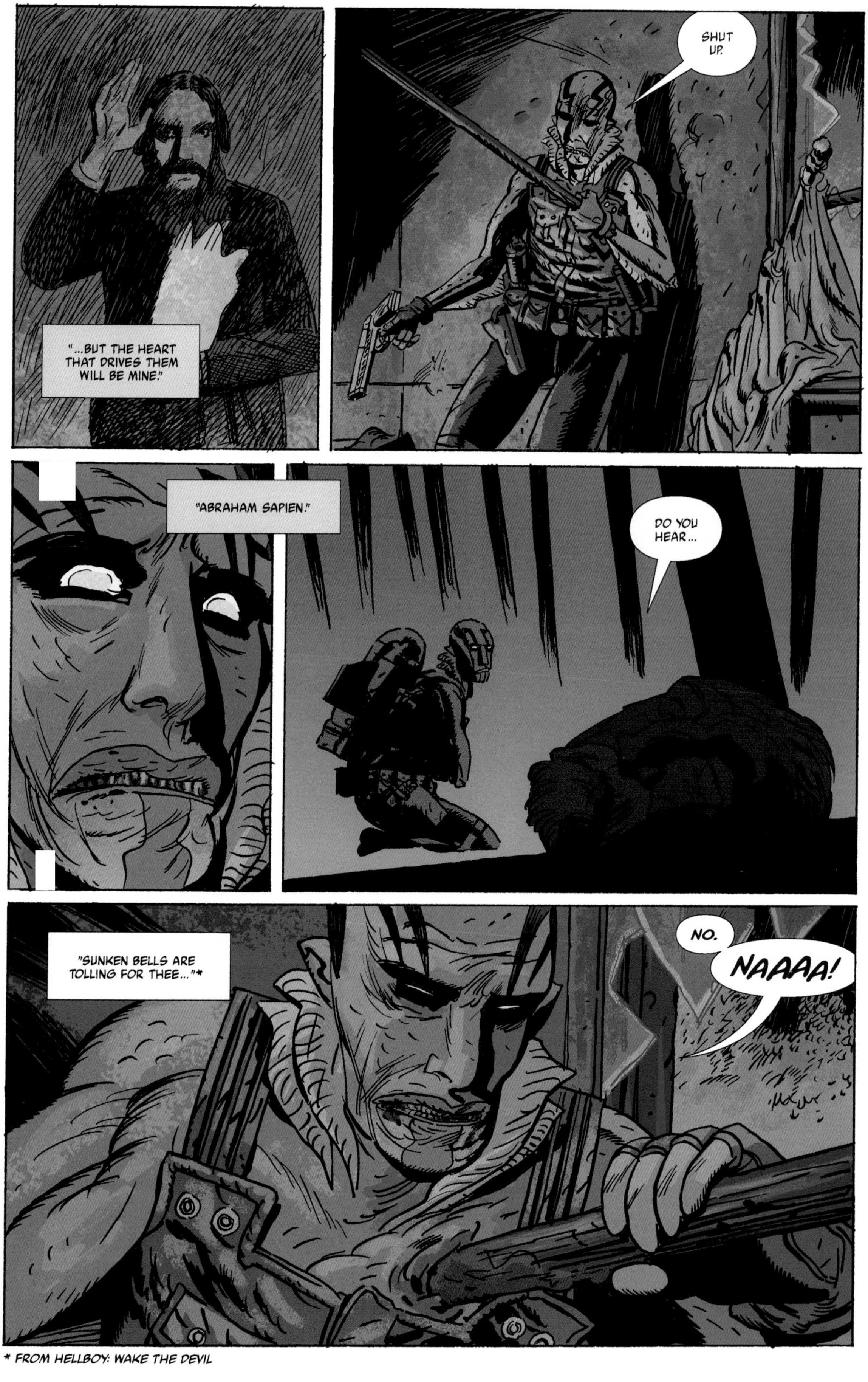
"...BUT THE HEART THAT DRIVES THEM WILL BE MINE."
SHUT UP.
"ABRAHAM SAPIEN."
DO YOU HEAR...
"SUNKEN BELLS ARE TOLLING FOR THEE..."*
NO.
NAAAA!

* FROM HELLBOY: WAKE THE DEVIL

AAAAAHH!

UGH!

UGH!

YOU STILL LIVE?

YOU LOVE THE PAIN SO MUCH?

YOU'RE HIM...

THE WEST VIRGINIA MIRACLE BOY.

YOU SEE, THE DRAGON HAS TAKEN MY YOUTH, MADE ME THIS OLD MAN.

WHY HAVE YOU DONE ALL THIS?

WHY?

I WAS *CHOSEN.*

AS RASPUTIN WAS CHOSEN, SO *I* WAS CHOSEN. UPON HIS DEATH IT FELL TO ME TO COMPLETE THE WORK.

AND NOW SADU-HEM IS GONE, CONSUMED BY THE SAME ELEMENTAL FIRE THAT DESTROYED HIM BEFORE.

SO WHAT WAS THE POINT?

THE DRAGON COMMANDS.

SADU-HEM WAS SPAWNED OF THE DRAGON...

"SADU-HEM WAS A GOD. HE RAISED HIMSELF OUT OF THE ASHES, OUT OF HIS OWN GRAVE, ONLY TO BE HELD A PRISONER...

"*I* SENT DERBY TO SET *HIM* FREE...

"*I* MADE IT POSSIBLE FOR HIM TO GO ABOUT, FOR A LITTLE WHILE, IN THE SHAPE OF A MAN...

"LONG ENOUGH TO PASS ON HIS GIFT TO THE WORLD."

POK

BECAUSE OF YOU ALL THOSE PEOPLE WERE--

SAVED...

NO!

"REBORN..."

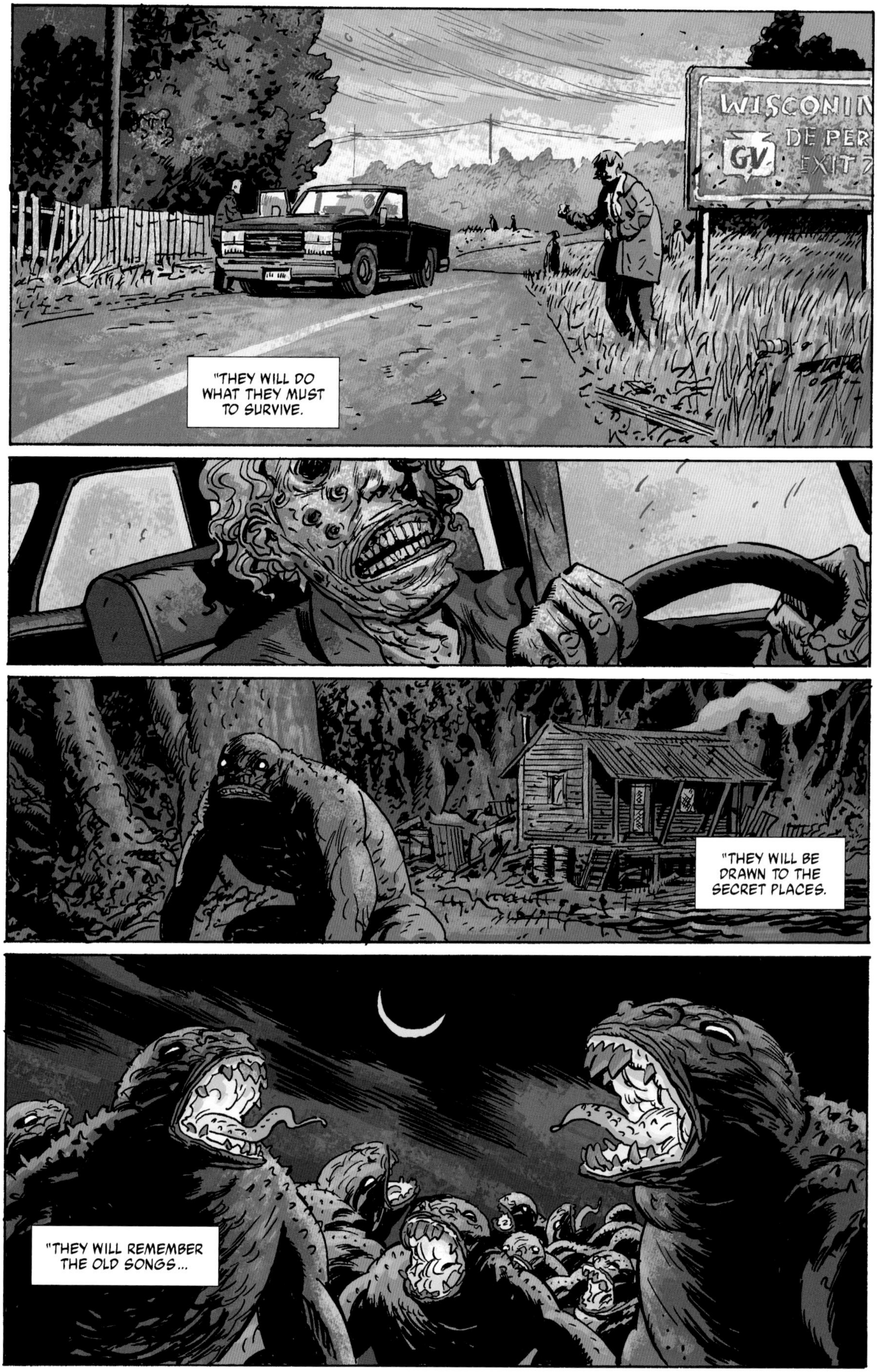
"THEY WILL DO WHAT THEY MUST TO SURVIVE.
"THEY WILL BE DRAWN TO THE SECRET PLACES.
"THEY WILL REMEMBER THE OLD SONGS...

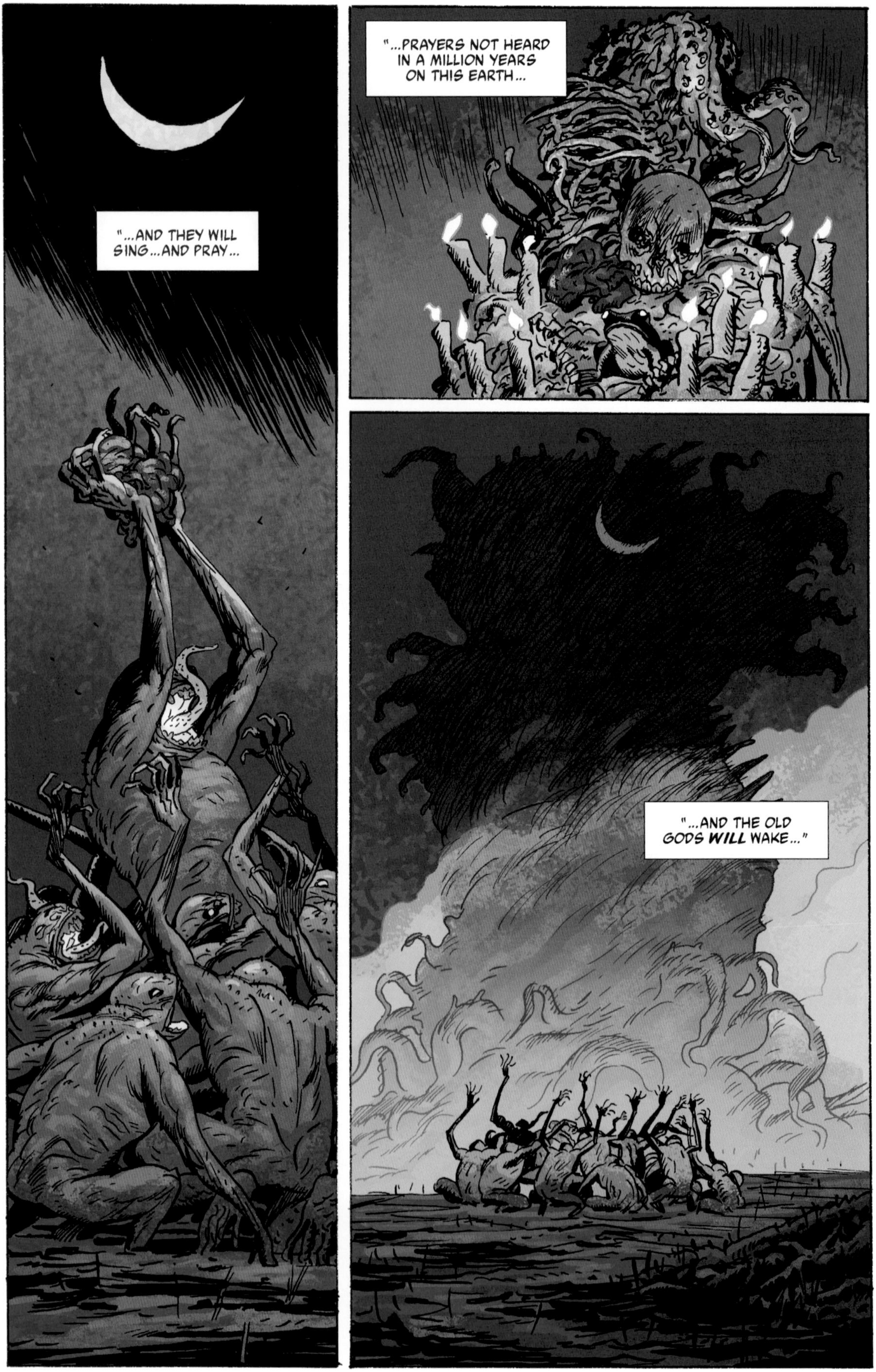
"...AND THEY WILL SING...AND PRAY...
"...PRAYERS NOT HEARD IN A MILLION YEARS ON THIS EARTH...
"...AND THE OLD GODS WILL WAKE..."

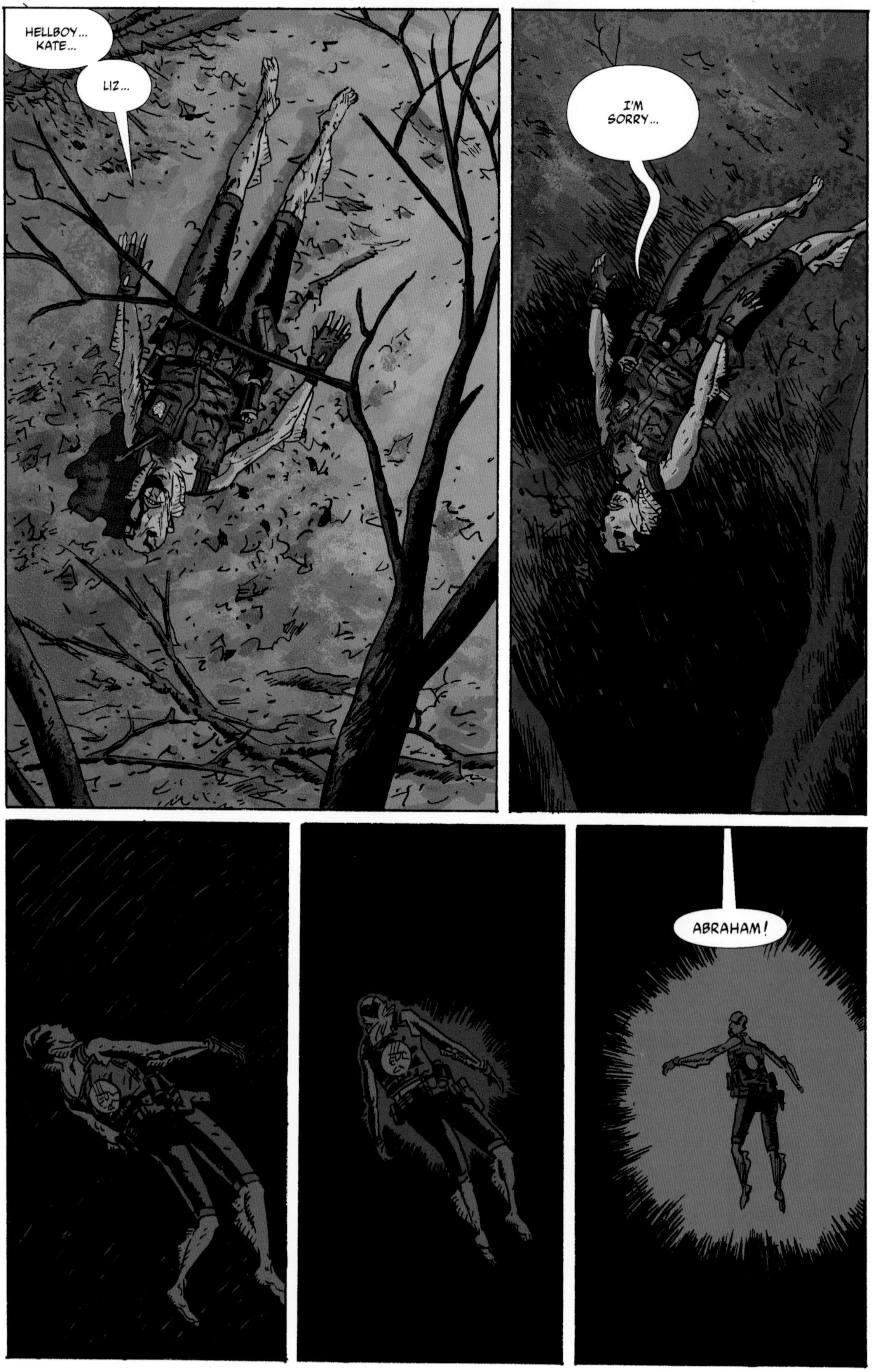
HELLBOY... KATE...
LIZ...
I'M SORRY...
ABRAHAM!

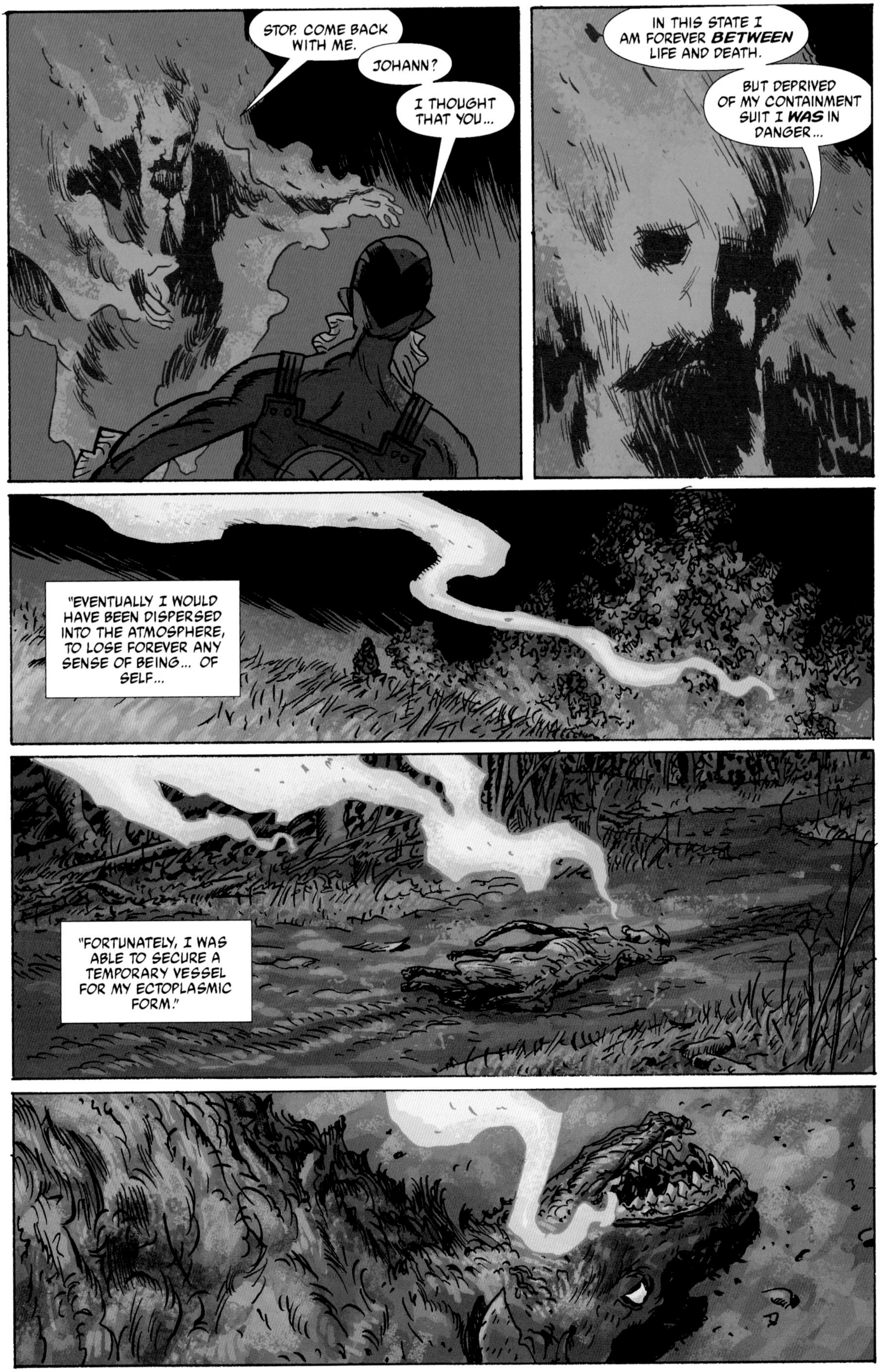
STOP. COME BACK WITH ME.
JOHANN?
I THOUGHT THAT YOU...
IN THIS STATE I AM FOREVER BETWEEN LIFE AND DEATH.
BUT DEPRIVED OF MY CONTAINMENT SUIT I WAS IN DANGER...
"EVENTUALLY I WOULD HAVE BEEN DISPERSED INTO THE ATMOSPHERE, TO LOSE FOREVER ANY SENSE OF BEING... OF SELF...
"FORTUNATELY, I WAS ABLE TO SECURE A TEMPORARY VESSEL FOR MY ECTOPLASMIC FORM."

BONG

ABE!

ABE, WHERE ARE YOU?

ABE?

OH MY--

HE IS GONE.

BONG

"THEY ARE
TOLLING
FOR ME.

"OUT OF THE
CAVERNS OF
NUM-YABISC...

"...DARK AND
TERRIBLE
DEEP...

"THE OCEAN IS
CALLING HER
CHILDREN HOME."

CHAPTER
FIVE

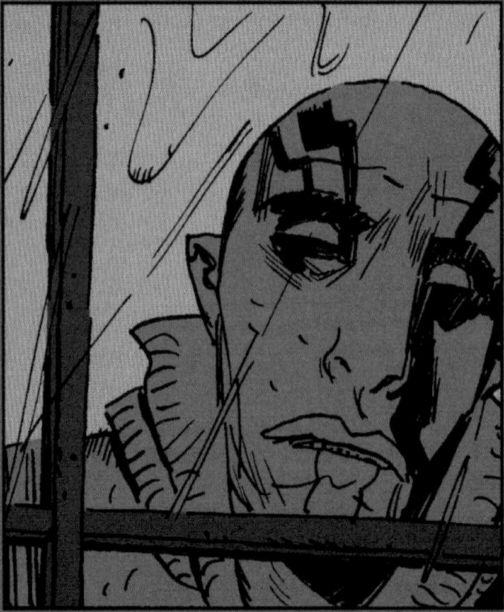

BONG

HE IS GONE.

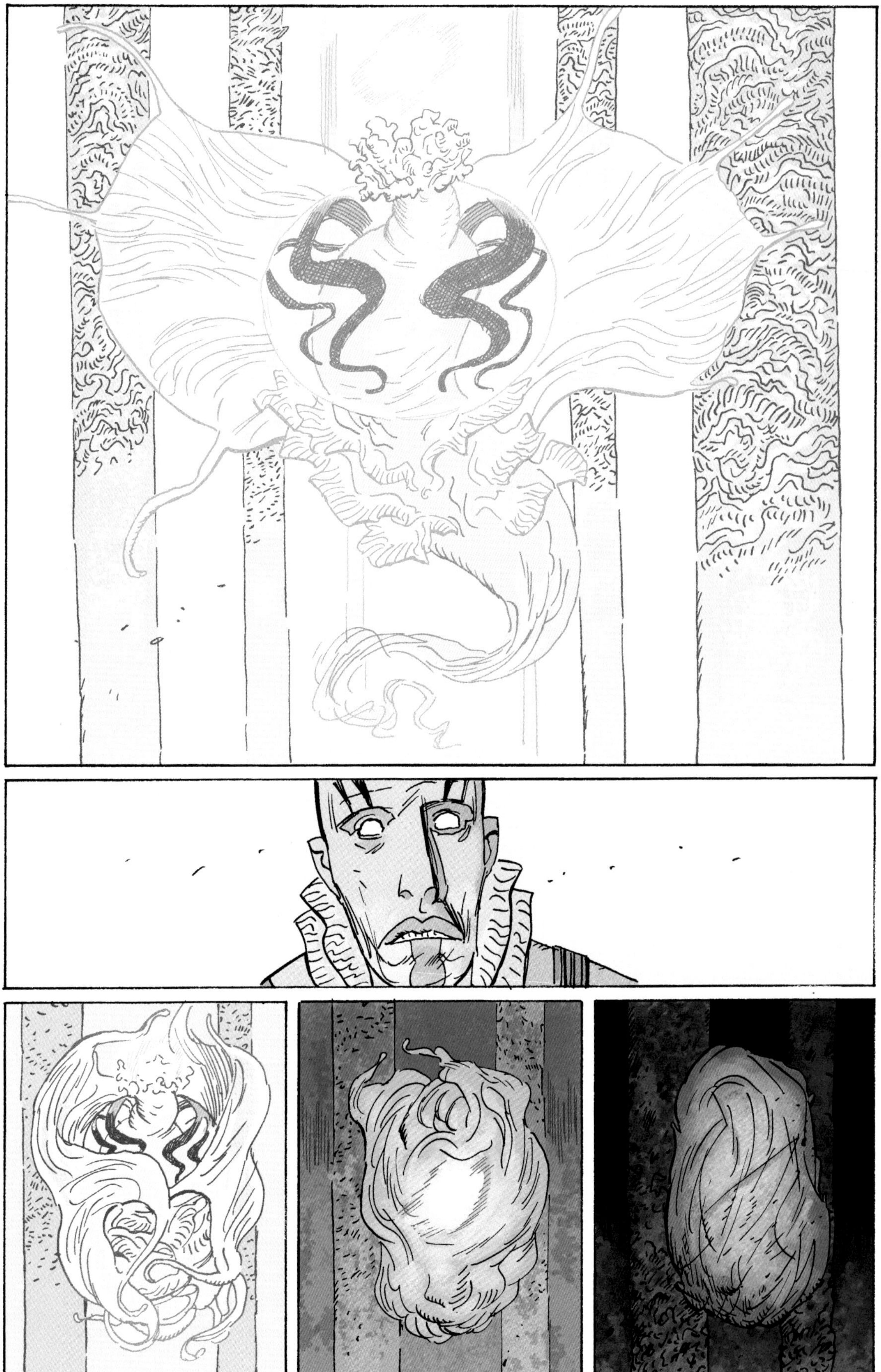

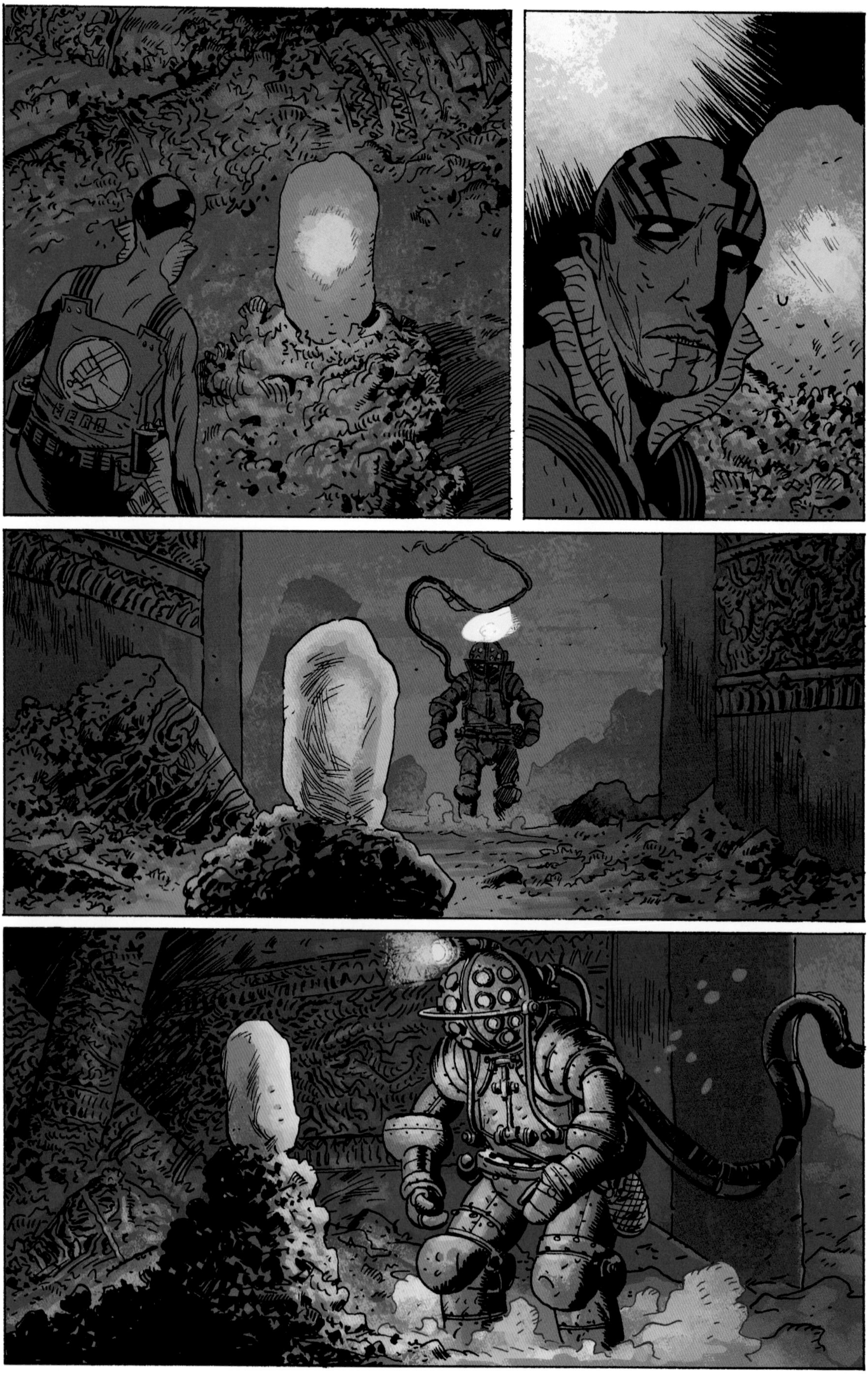

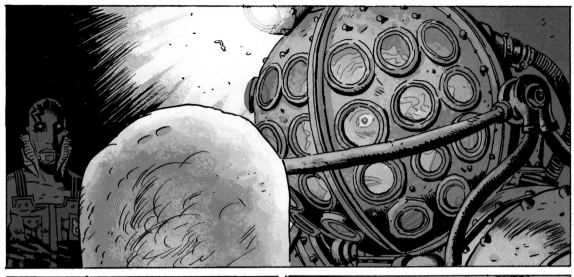

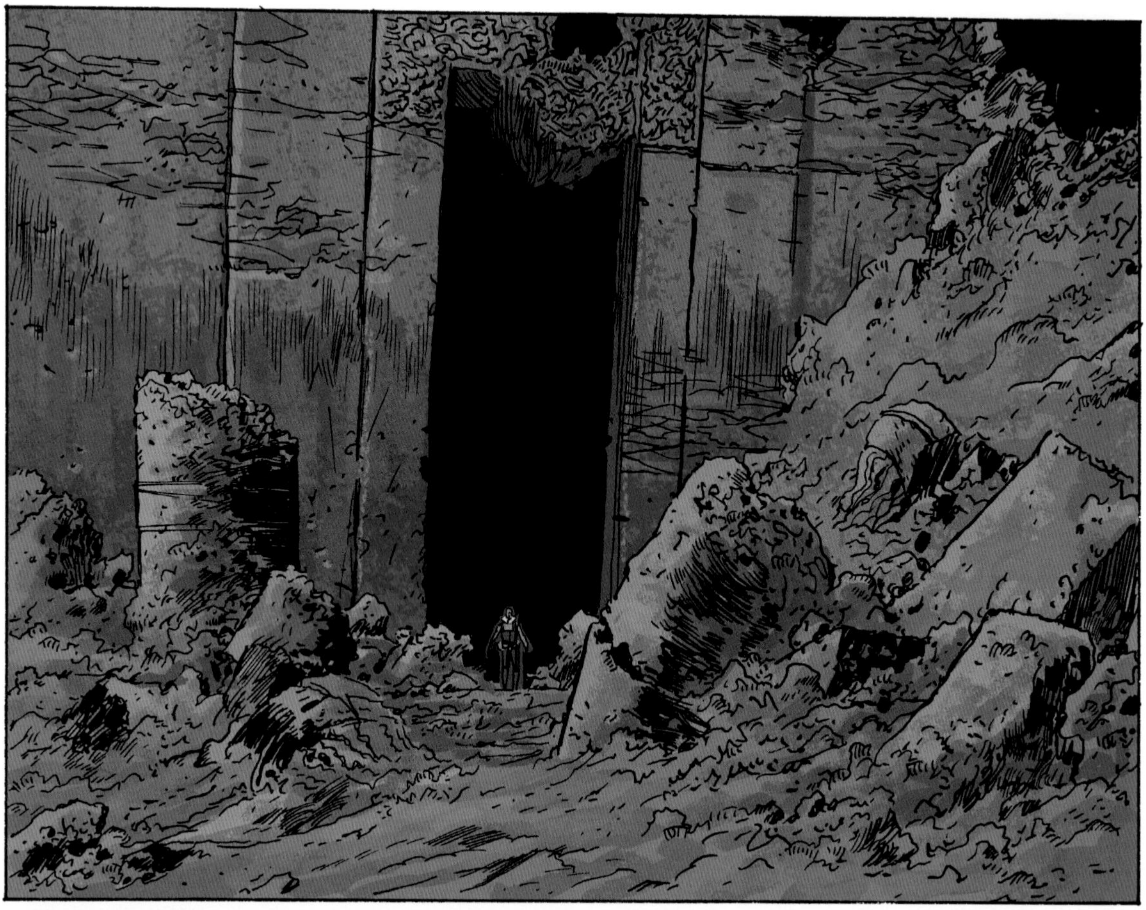

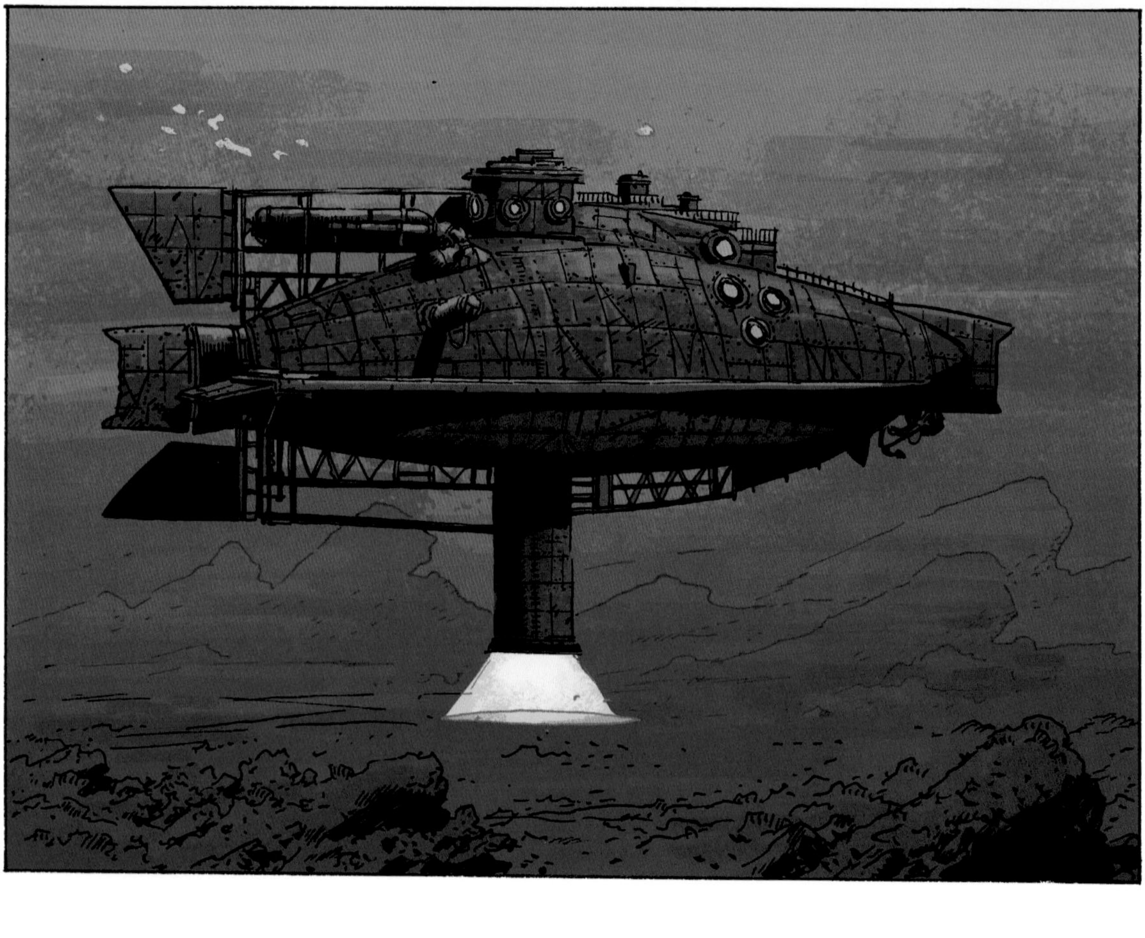

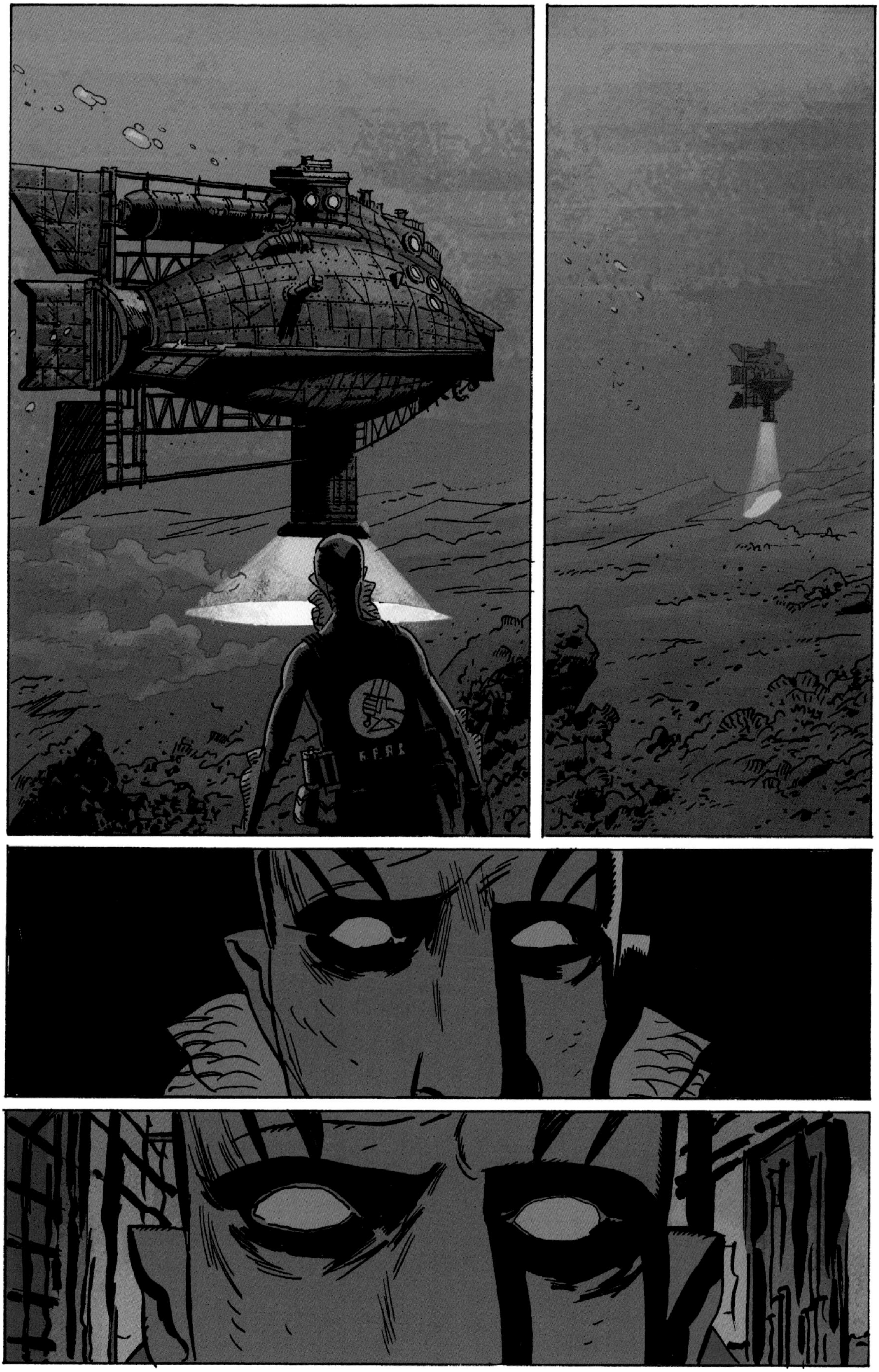

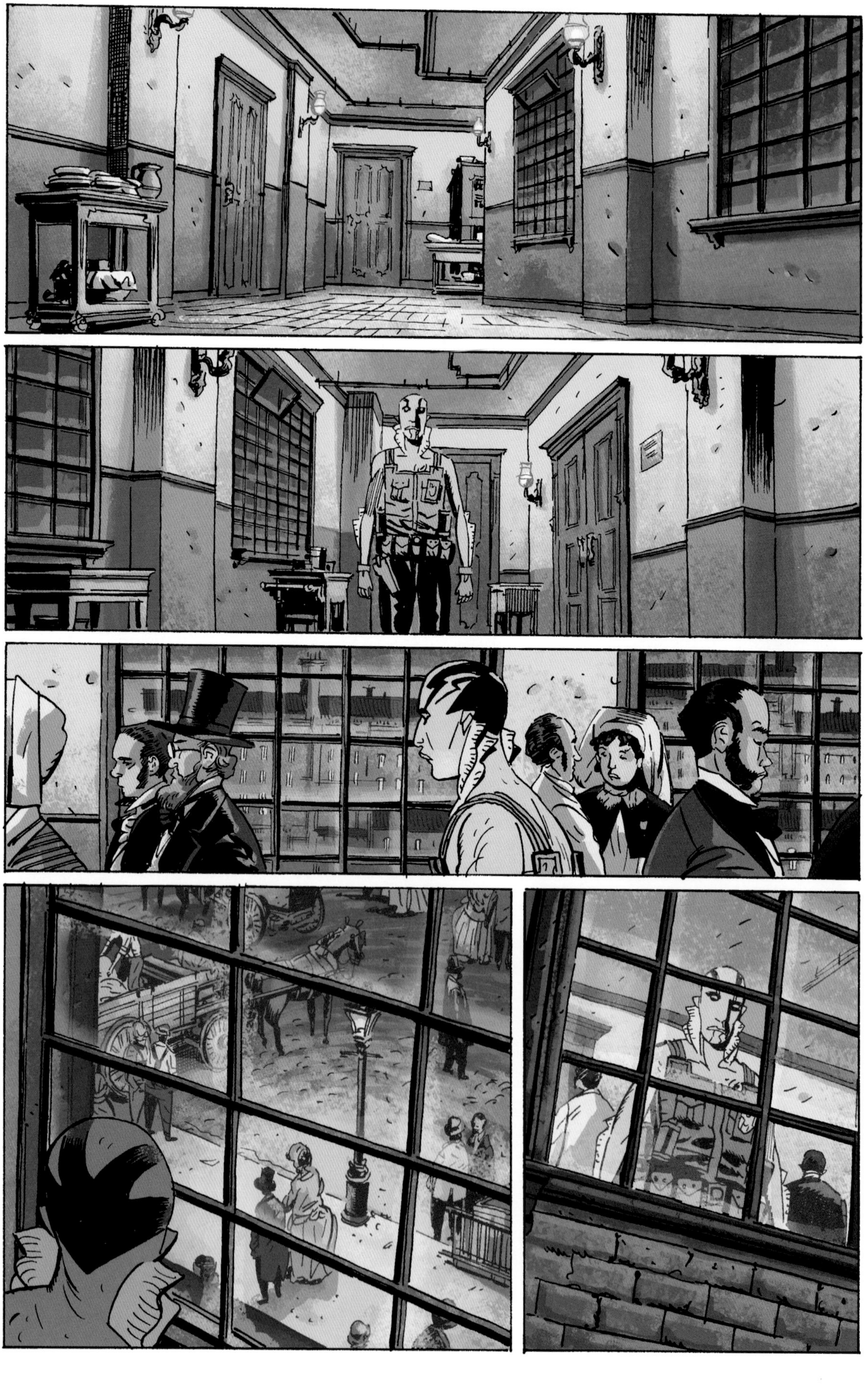

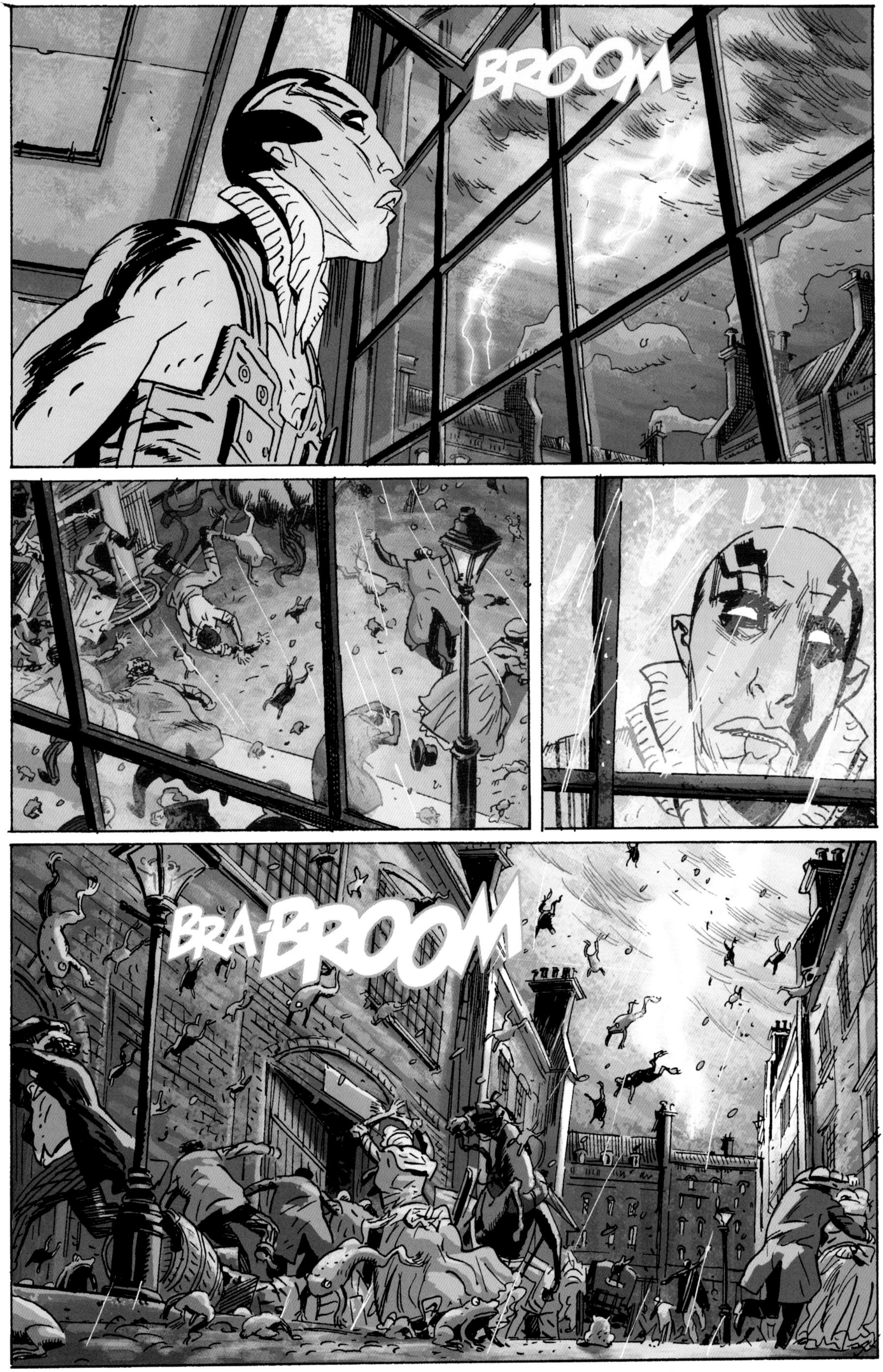
BROOM
BRA-BROOM

SPLAP

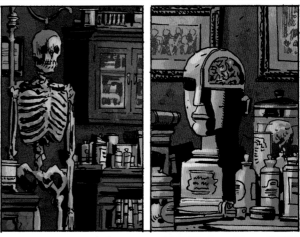

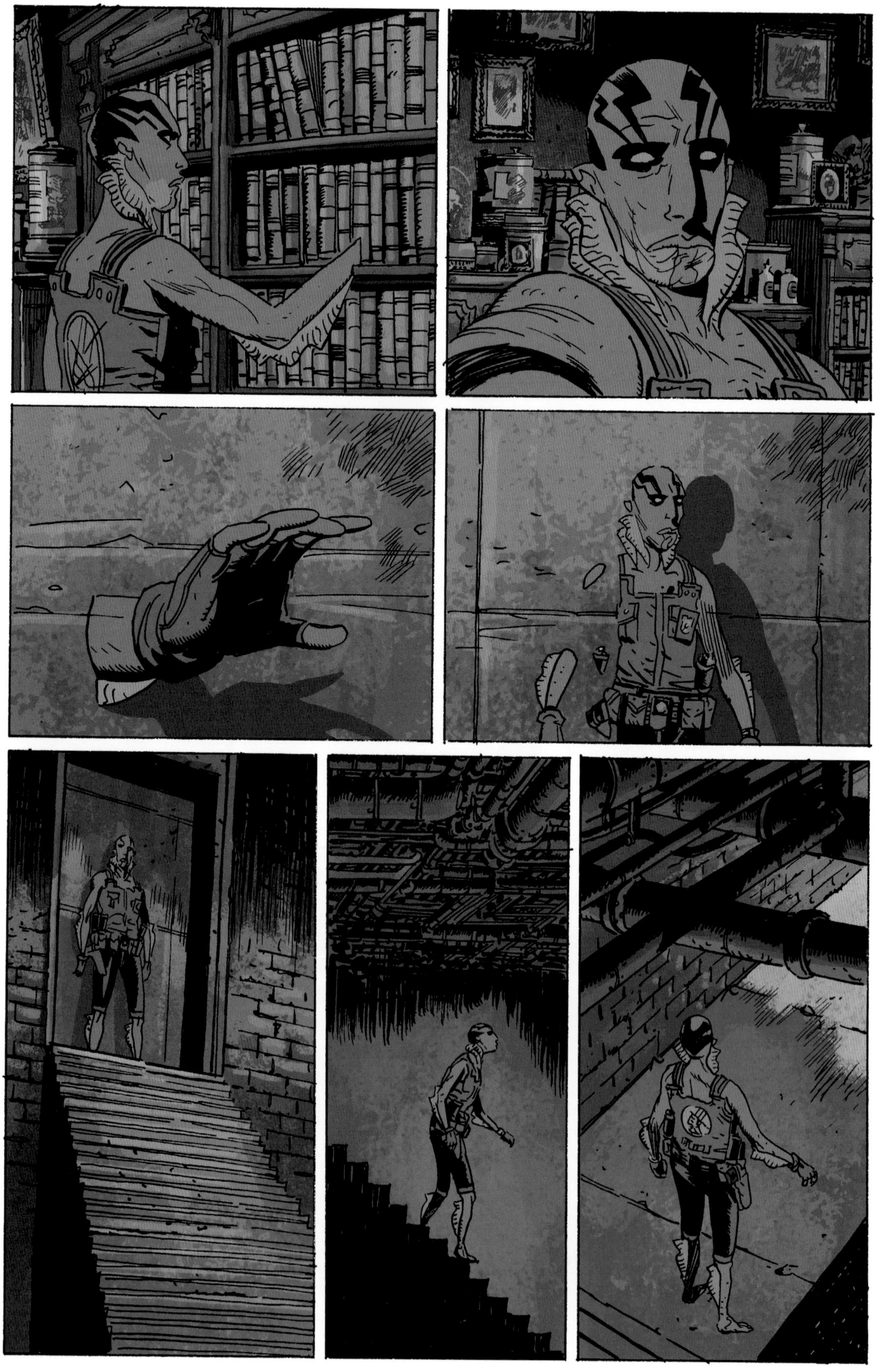

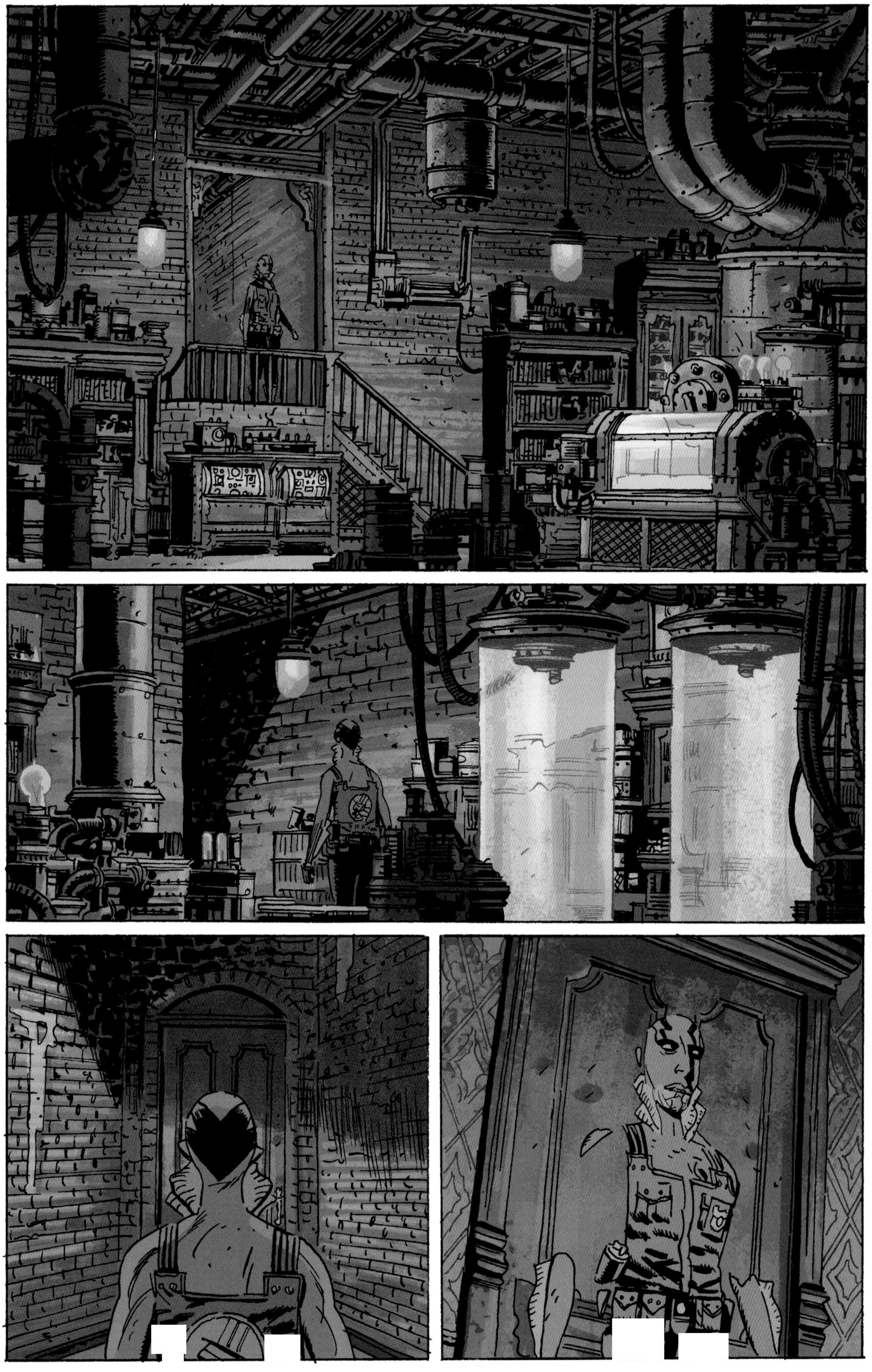

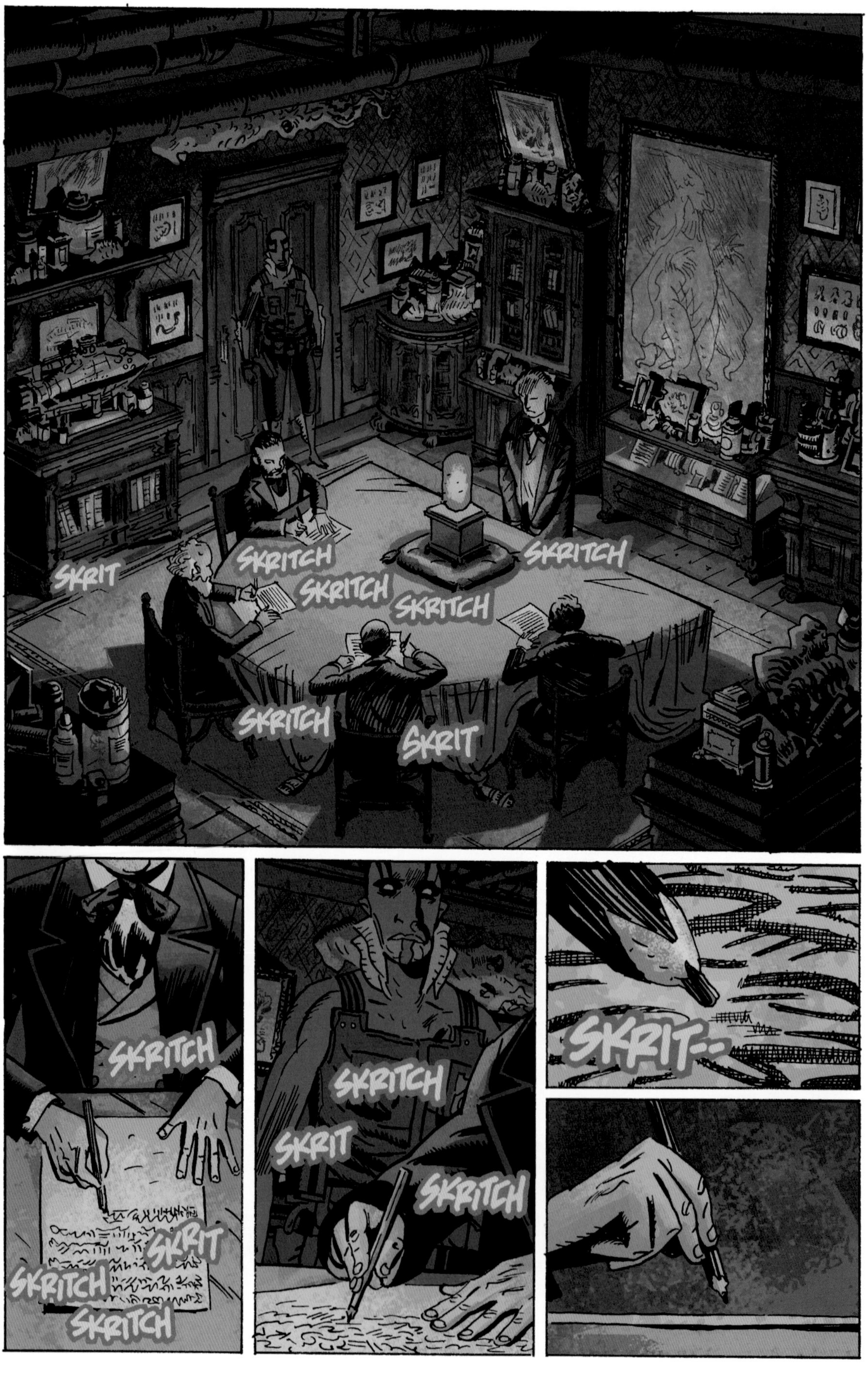
SKRIT
SKRITCH
SKRITCH
SKRITCH
SKRITCH
SKRITCH
SKRIT
SKRITCH
SKRIT
SKRITCH
SKRITCH
SKRITCH
SKRIT
SKRITCH
SKRIT--

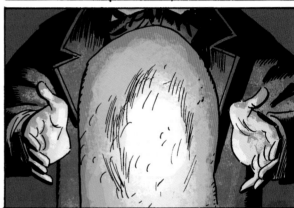

UGHURRAAGAGA UMAA UTHU
GAA ATHEMM UGATHAAAR
UGUGURATHAAAM UTH E MM
UGG ATHAAA AGATHAA
ETT URAAA...

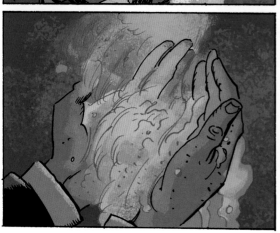

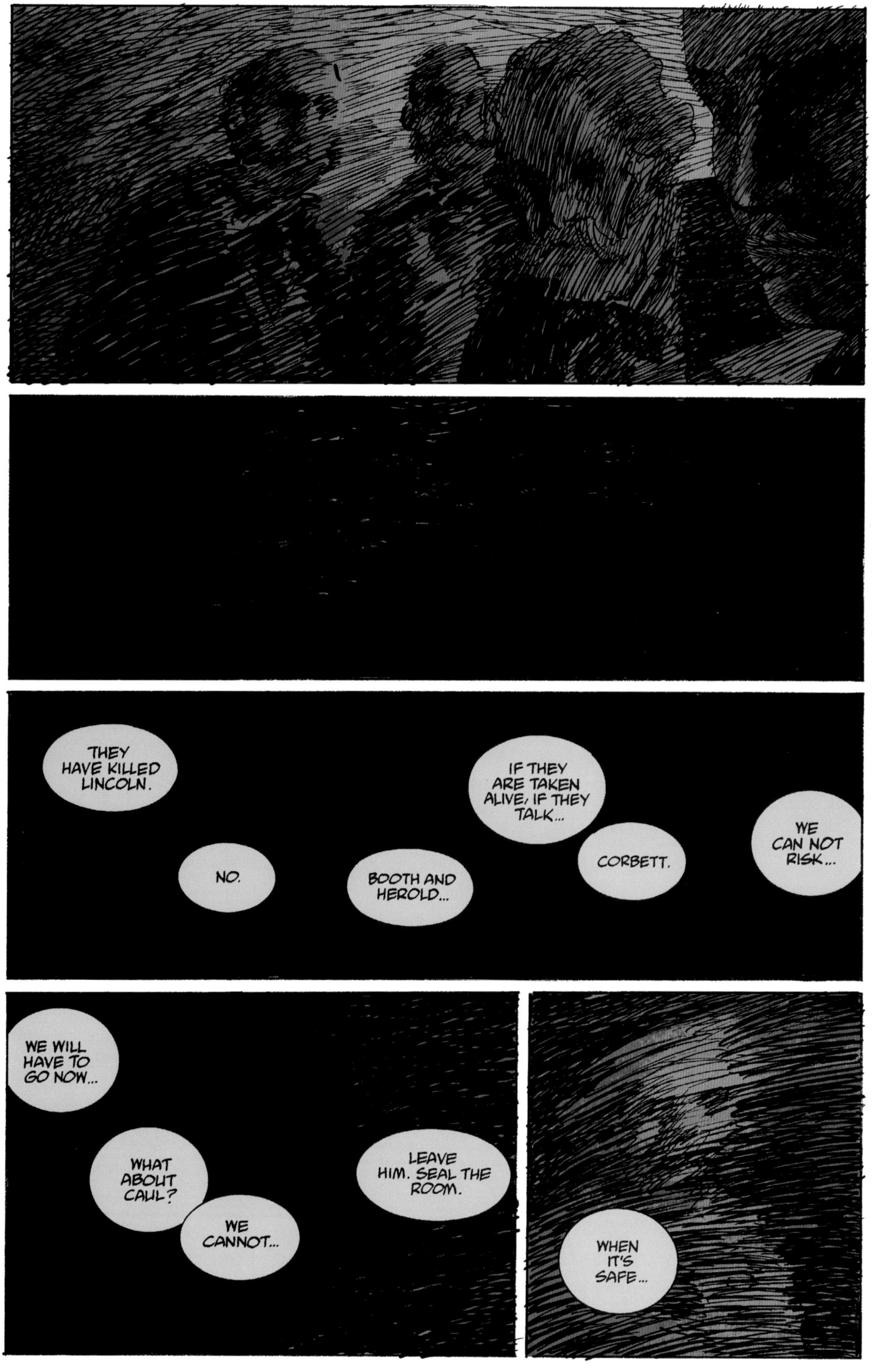
THEY HAVE KILLED LINCOLN.
NO.
BOOTH AND HEROLD...
IF THEY ARE TAKEN ALIVE, IF THEY TALK...
CORBETT.
WE CAN NOT RISK...
WE WILL HAVE TO GO NOW...
WHAT ABOUT CAUL?
WE CANNOT...
LEAVE HIM. SEAL THE ROOM.
WHEN IT'S SAFE...

"WE'LL COME BACK FOR HIM."

WHAT?!

ABE!

BUT HE WAS...

WHAT...

WHAT AM I?

HE'S DELIRIOUS.

DON'T WORRY, MISS CORRIGAN. THE HOSPITAL IN ROCKLAND IS STANDING BY.

SON OF A...

RURP

RURP

RAAARP

RARP RARP

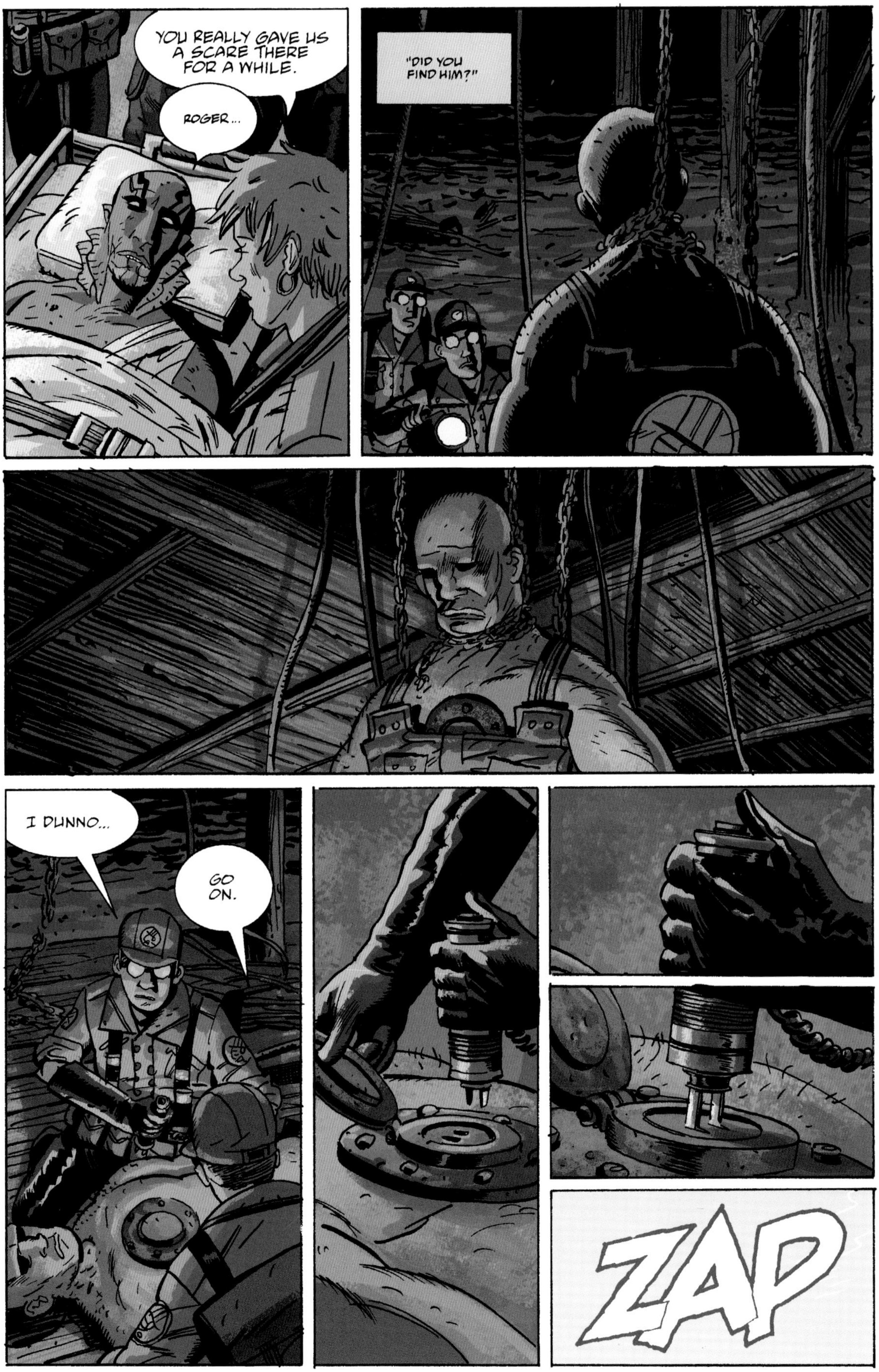
YOU REALLY GAVE US A SCARE THERE FOR A WHILE.
ROGER...
"DID YOU FIND HIM?"
I DUNNO...
GO ON.
ZAP

AFTERWORD

The first B.P.R.D. book, *Hollow Earth*, was something of an experiment. We wanted to see if we could expand on the Hellboy world with a story that didn't have Hellboy in it. It worked, and we were all very happy. The next book, *The Soul of Venice & Other Stories*, was another successful experiment, allowing four different creative teams (five if you count the short story by Cameron Stewart and myself) to tell stand-alone B.P.R.D. adventures. But for this third book we—editor Scott Allie and I—wanted something different. We wanted to start a new, ongoing line of books, to treat the B.P.R.D. the same way I've been treating Hellboy all these years. So we needed something big to kick that off.

Back when I was drawing the first *Hellboy* series, even as I was destroying the pseudo-Lovecraftian god-monster Sadu-Hem, I was thinking he should come back some day—as a tiny fungus that works its way into a guy through a bullet hole causing him to swell up into something horrible that eventually escapes into a graveyard where it reanimates a bunch of rotting skeletons. Of course. Add to that the vampire-like man-frogs and Rasputin's promise that Abe Sapien would get speared to death, and the story started to take shape. But there was something missing. Fortunately, during filming of the *Hellboy* movie in Prague, I got hit with the flu (the scary-ass Eastern European kind) and was ordered to spend four days in my hotel room. Sweating and hallucinating, deprived of all human contact, I spent those ninety-six hours trying to come up with an ending for *Plague of Frogs*.

And I did.

The Secret Origin of Abe Sapien

Over the years I've toyed with the idea of working Abe's origin into a story. Trouble is, I sort of liked Abe not having an origin. I loved

that he was just discovered in a jar in the basement. But I also loved the origin I'd come up with, and knew it added a new dimension to the character. And when I found a way for Abe to not only witness his origin, but actually participate in it—when I saw that by solving one mystery we were actually presenting an even bigger one—then I knew it was okay to finally tell the tale. But who do you get to draw something like that?

Guy Davis

What can I say? I've been following Guy's work for years—*Phantom Stranger*, *Sandman Mystery Theater*, *Nevermen*, and his own brilliant *Marquis* series. I am constantly amazed by his ability to draw anything and everything, apparently with little or no effort. He is a master of both clutter and understatement and is, in my humble opinion, the best "creature guy" in the business. So who better to draw the origin of Abe Sapien? Who better to kick off this whole new direction for the B.P.R.D.? I only hope that the promise of Victorian submarines and tenticular monsters will keep Guy around for a very long time.

There you go …

MIKE MIGNOLA

Mike Mignola
New York City

B.P.R.D.

SKETCHBOOK

The following pages contain drawings and character designs by Guy Davis, with notes from the artist. The practice drawings on this page were done to get the feel of the characters.

Mike's description for a "fungus elephant-man" instantly put that connotation in my head and in early designs.

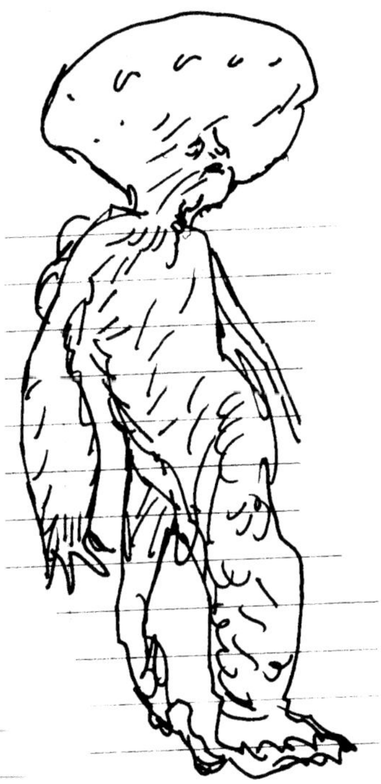

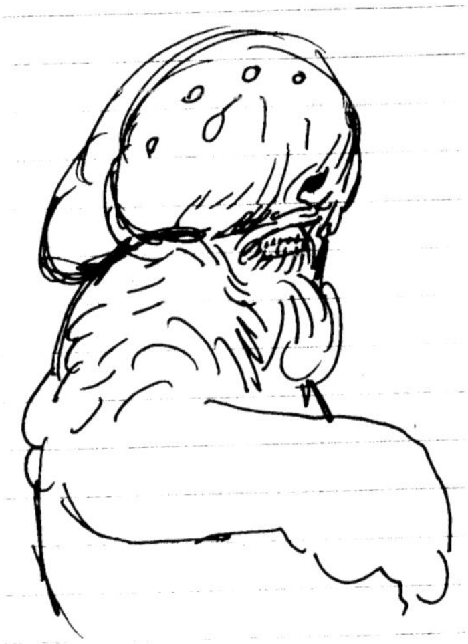

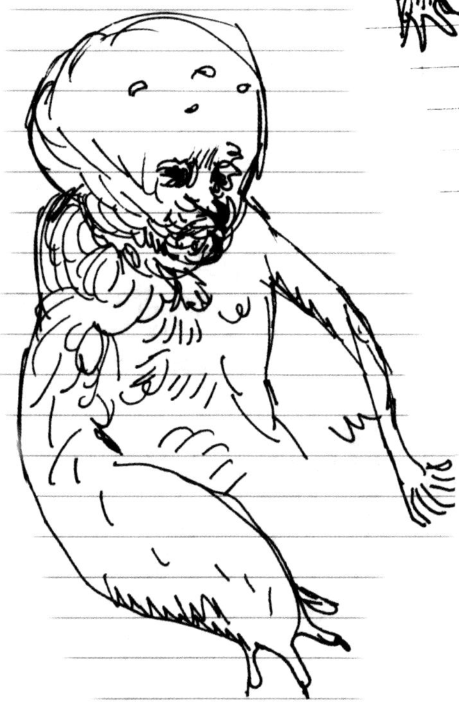

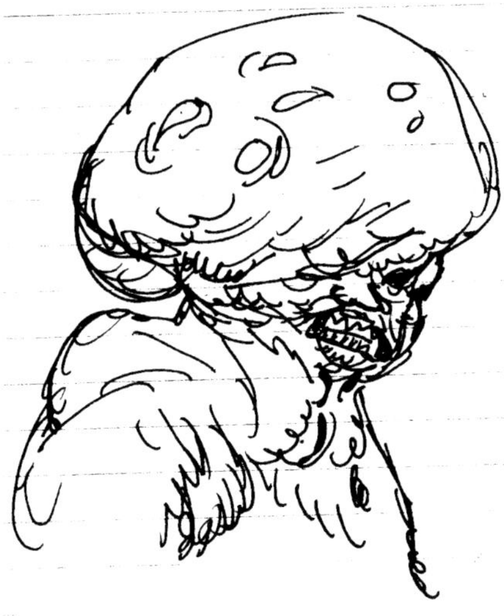

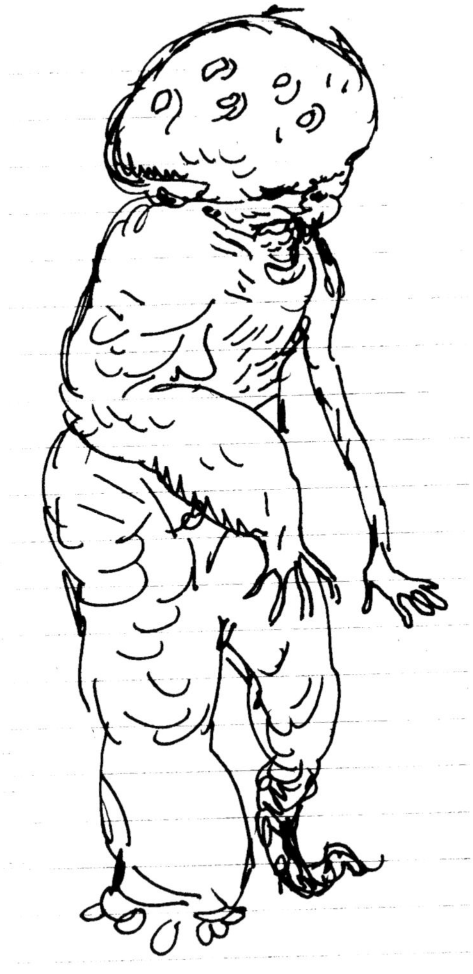

Early "jellyfish" designs for the entity from Chapter 5—the final version [opposite] incorporated some of Abe's design markings and gills.

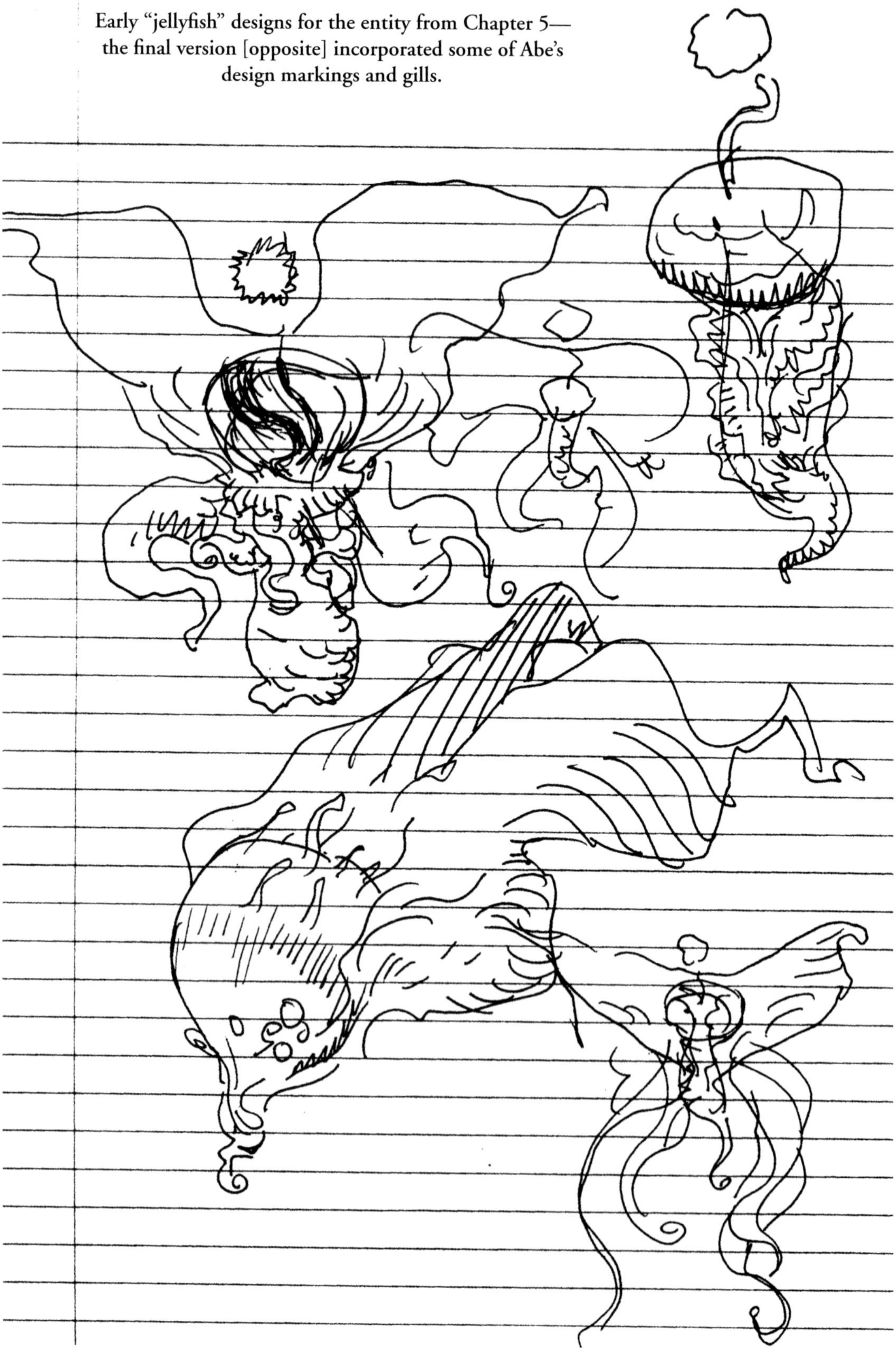

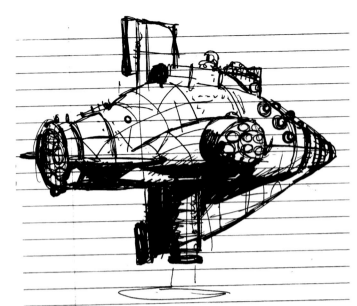

The Victorian submarine went through a number of different versions in both sketches and in the finished pencils with a lot of brilliant ideas from Mike [opposite] finally bringing it all together.

OIL SLICK

OIL SLICK

EXTENDED LIGHT AROUND ABE

GOING UP — STRAIGHT AWAY

TURNING RIGHT

TILT BACK AND SWING

LIGHT SMALLER

MORE FISH LIKE/ LOOSE TOP RUDDER

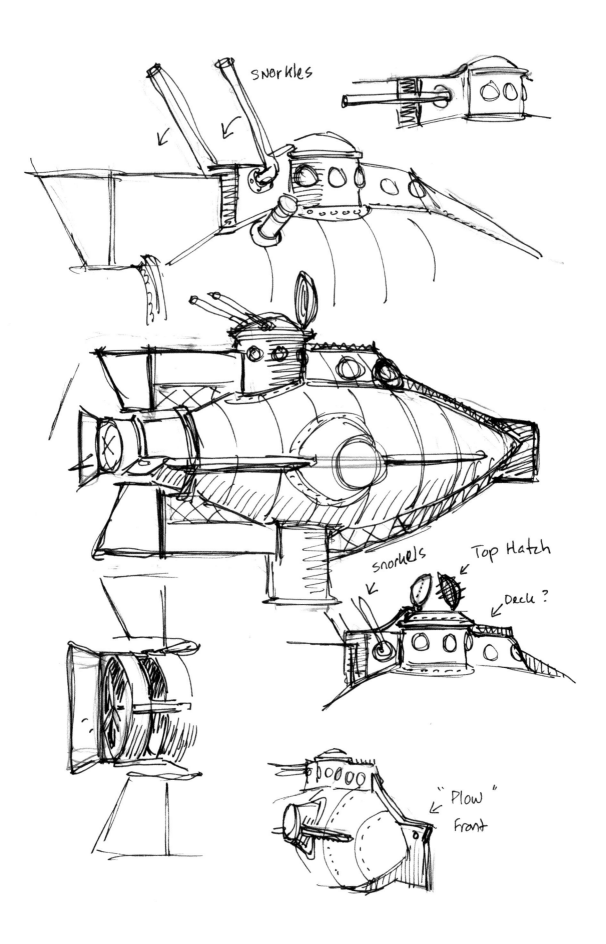

snorkles

snorkels

snorkels

Top Hatch

Deck ?

"Plow" front

SLICK BACK
ON TOP

VICTORIAN
ABE

FULL
AT
BOTTOM

For "Victorian Abe," or Caul,
I tried to keep the basic shape
and facial features of Abe Sapien
recognizable for his past human
form. On the left, another
commissioned drawing of Abe
and Liz, pursued by zombies.

BPRD #5

(14)

— Page 23

- Panel 1 – Abe on gurney looks up at Kate and asks about Roger. Kate Looks grim.
- Panel 2 – Cut to a couple agents entering the boat house where we last saw Roger.
- Panel 3 – Agents find Roger hanging. Looks dead.
- Panel 4 – They lower Dead Roger onto the floor.
- Panel 5 – Agent opens Roger's chest plate with one hand. It isn't a black hole but there's ~~[illegible]~~ an outlet in there. In ~~this~~ Agent's other hand he has some device with prongs.
- Panel 6 – Either close up of Prongs going into outlet or thumb pressing button on device (or both) –
- Final Panel is just sound effect "ZAP"

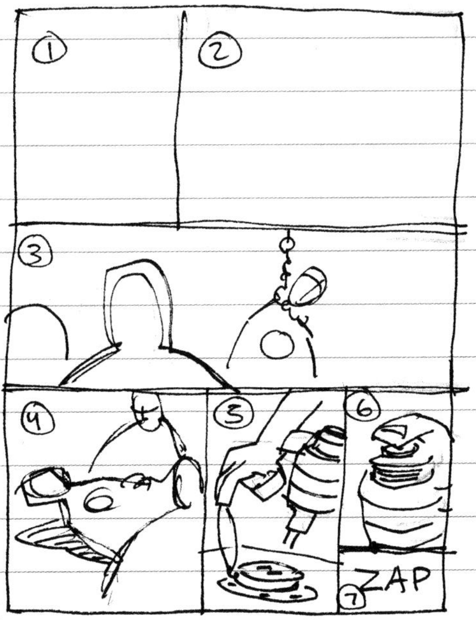

1
2
3
4
5
6
ZAP
7

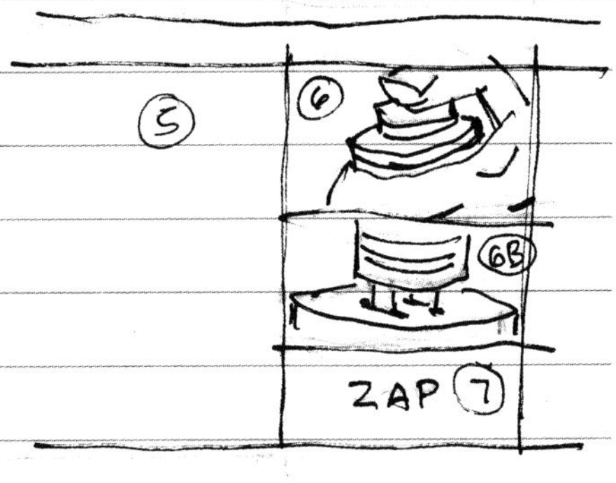

5
6
6B
ZAP
7

A sample of Mike's script and thumbnails, from the second-to-last page of the story. Often Mike would breakdown certain scenes that he had a specific pacing in mind for—to give it that Mignola flow—and then add the final dialogue after seeing the finished art.
—Guy Davis
Crab Point, Michigan

HELLBOY

by MIKE MIGNOLA

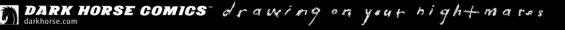